LEWIS JR. HIGH SCHOOL
VANCOUVER PUBLIC SCHOOLS

☑ CO-API-139

78-21872

780	Willson, Robina
Wil	Beckles
	The voice of music

FEB 8 '83	DATE DUE	

VANCOUVER SCHOOL DISTRICT #37

The Voice of Music

Robina Beckles Willson

The Voice of Music

Foreword by Yehudi Menuhin
Illustrated by Jeroo Roy

A MARGARET K. MC ELDERRY BOOK

Atheneum   1977   New York

Library of Congress Cataloging in Publication Data

Willson, Robina Beckles.
The voice of music.

"A Margaret K. McElderry book."
SUMMARY: Discusses the wide range of classical, pop,
and mechanical music and the instruments used in
music-making.
1. Music—Juvenile literature. [1. Music.
2. Musical instruments] I. Roy, Jeroo. II. Title.
ML3930.A2W56   780   77–3225
ISBN 0–689–50096–3

Copyright © 1976 by Robina Beckles Willson
All rights reserved
Manufactured in the United States of America by
Halliday Lithograph Corporation
West Hanover, Massachusetts

First American Edition

For Judith, with love and thanks

Contents

Foreword by Yehudi Menuhin

Teacher and student will find that this book covers a very wide range of musical subjects. "The Voice of Music" provides an endless source of themes, musical and otherwise, to be illustrated, songs to be sung, instruments of various cultures to be investigated, manuscripts to be studied, recordings of folk music, as for instance the Unesco series and the Nonesuch Explorer Series, to be listened to, and films to be viewed.

In fact, the value of this book lies in the improvisation it will inspire in the teacher and in the stimulation it will provide in the young reader.

6 January 1975

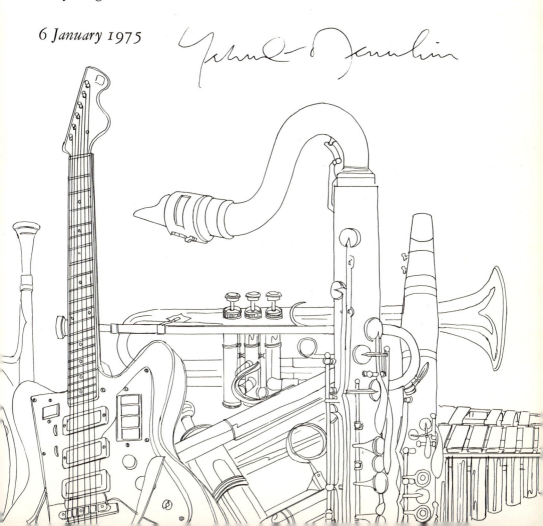

Preface

Here is a book to guide you in finding out more about music. It will introduce you to as many of music's voices as possible. The range is deliberately wide, so that you can gain some idea of all there is to know. You will find strange and exotic instruments alongside the better known ones, and will come to see some surprising connections between widely different ways of making music. In one book details have to be limited, but you will be able to choose which voice attracts you the most and then to focus your playing, listening and reading in the years to come.

There is so much to enjoy. Music will overflow into every part of your life: singing and dancing, working and worshipping. Today's music embraces the international world of pop as well as a continuing development of the classical patterns of earlier centuries. And today's musicians are inspired afresh by that traditional music which was not written out, but passed down from generation to generation.

Music involves the arts of a composer, a performer, and a listener. "The Voice of Music" is a first guide to all three, and to a range of interest and pleasure which can absorb you for a lifetime.

Many people have given me help and information, but in particular I should like to thank John Andrewes, director of the Finchley Children's Music Group; staff at Australia House; Mark Beckles Willson; Krishna Biltoo; Wendy Bird, Primary Music Organiser, Inner London Education Authority; Dr Richard Clothier; Bruce Cole; Audrey Dennett, Music Inspector, Inner London Education Authority; N. Gandy, the Keswick Museum; Jan Haymer; staff at the Horniman Museum; Dr John Paynter, the Department of Music, York University; Jeroo Roy; John Shirley-Quirk; Madeau Stewart, Producer, B.B.C., Sound Archive Production Unit; and Fritz Spiegl.

I am deeply indebted to Catherine Burchill, who encouraged and advised me while typing the whole manuscript with meticulous care.

R. B. W.
Twickenham 1975

1 The Human Voice

THE HUMAN VOICE is the instrument which we all have from birth. And, though it may only be the mother who finds a baby's first lamblike cries music in her ears, that sound is the first step towards singing.

Of all the creatures on the earth, only man and birds seem to sing, that is to create tunes and rhythmic patterns. Birds sing to claim territory, to pay court, to communicate with other birds. Man does that by talking. For him, singing is a special form of self-expression. No group, however primitive, has been discovered which has no singing or chanting to call its own. It seems a natural activity to sing, and you may notice younger children humming with pleasure as they eat, or making up little chants with words they like, repeating them endlessly, with great satisfaction. That happens long before they are "taught" songs or rhymes.

It is as though we have two voices. One is for talking, one for singing. You can say a sentence or you can sing it. To sing the words requires a different effort. You seem to have to lift up your voice, quite literally. The effort you make is physical and mental. The sound that emerges from your mouth is your individual "voice". Speaking or singing, nobody else's is exactly the same. You can observe the personal qualities of people's voices by listening to them on the radio or the telephone, when no expression or movement adds to what they are saying. The voice speaks for itself.

A famous professional singer, John Shirley-Quirk, has tried to explain his own distinctive voice by saying that the voice *is* the person. "It is the whole of you that sings." So while the sounds he can produce are what he has trained himself to do, by technique, his actual singing in his own voice will be affected by the state of his health, what he feels about the music, and the type and mood of the audience listening to him.

Crying is nearer to singing than to speaking. There is a special sort of wailing lament which in Ireland is called keening, and used when mourning, to express and release grief. Equally, people sing for joy, and for delight in the sound they can make. Listen to giant football crowds.

The human voice is the only musical instrument which is all

alive. The balance of physical working and mental instructing by the singer to his own voice is almost impossible to describe. There remains a vital mystery, that responsive spirit which gives the voice its quality. The singer cannot say exactly how it is done. We can only describe the physical parts of this instrument which sings, making a sound as different from talking as dancing is from walking.

HOW WE SING

The human voice is a wind instrument in three main parts: a compressor of air (our breath), a vibrator, and a resonator. The compressor is our lungs. The vibrator is our vocal cords, set in a larynx or voice box within the throat. The resonator is in a way the whole body, but most especially the hollow parts of the neck, within the mouth and nose.

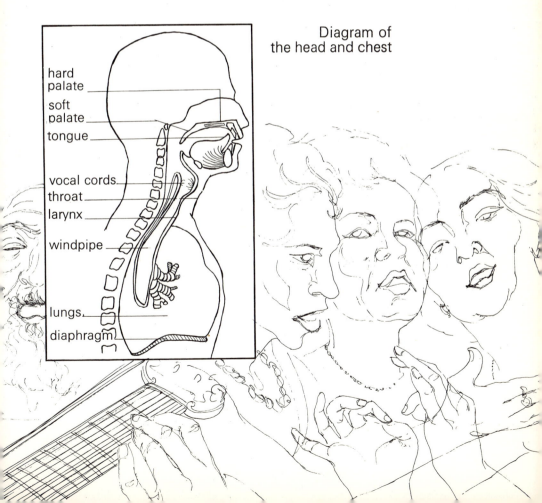

Diagram of
the head and chest

hard palate
soft palate
tongue
vocal cords
throat
larynx
windpipe
lungs
diaphragm

Breathing

The diaphragm separates the chest from the stomach and other organs of the abdomen and is muscular, so that it can be raised up into a dome, or rest flat. If you watch a tiny baby yelling hard, you will see the effect of its stomach and diaphragm hard at work.

Children and adults naturally use the expansion of the rib-cage, that is chest expansion, in breathing. But a singer will learn, with practice, to use his diaphragm, which is a lighter mechanism to control, and, naturally, more flexible than the *bones* of the ribs. So breathing by conscious use of the diaphragm is better for singing, because his control of it can be finer than over his rib-cage.

Our lungs work automatically. When we breathe in, the diaphragm flattens and causes the lungs to take in air, filling the space which has been made. The air sacs in the lungs expand outwards towards the walls of the chest, like full sponges. When the diaphragm relaxes and arches up again, the air is pushed out through nose and mouth, and the lungs shrink to their normal size.

This is basically how we breathe, and provide air for speaking and singing.

Breathing in
Breathing out

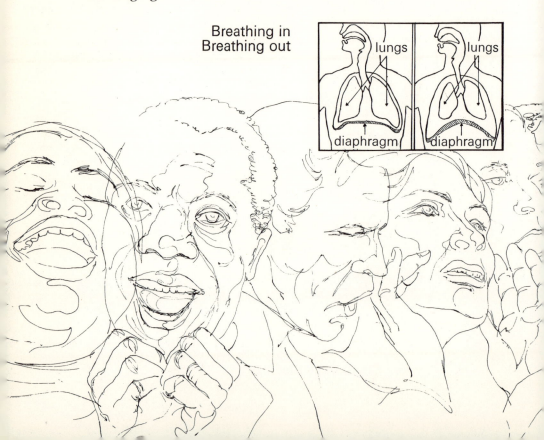

Making Sounds

Sounds are made by the movements of the vocal cords, which, as with reeds in a wind instrument, vibrate, and change the air taken in into sound waves. The windpipe is a hollow tube about five inches long, ending with the larynx, a hollow framework of cartilages. Two small muscular bands, the cords, about half an inch long in a man, and less in a woman or child, jut out, looking rather like that ligament which joins the tongue to the floor of the mouth. The gap between the cords is called the glottis. The cords take on a V shape when we breathe in, and draw close when vibrating and sounding a note.

We do not control the vocal cords by will. As a singer thinks of the note he wants to sound, the cords adjust themselves automatically to the right length and tension to produce that sound.

The shape of the mouth controls the vowel which comes out. Sing "ah, eye, ee, oo and oh" into the mirror, and see how your lips and tongue change position as they amplify your notes. The sound is reverberating in your mouth and nose. You can understand why head colds are particularly trying for singers.

Larynx and vocal cords as seen from above

vocal cords   larynx

Singing Well

What makes a good singer? A few people seem to have a natural talent before training, but most singers admit a great debt to their teachers. There is a crucial reason for this. A singer does not hear his own voice as others do. He cannot. What he receives is a physical sensation from making certain sounds.

This is because he hears his voice largely through bone conduction. The sounds which start inside his body are transmitted directly to the inner ear by the sympathetic vibration of certain bones. A violinist also experiences this to a lesser degree, hearing his violin through vibrations in the collar bone, in contact with his instrument.

The normal way of hearing is by movement of air. Briefly, sound waves enter the ear passage and beat on a membrane at its end, called the ear-drum. Then the vibrations cross a chain of three small bones in the middle ear cavity to reach the inner ear.

When a singer hears himself on a record or tape, he may not at first even recognize his own voice. The nearest way to hearing yourself as others do is to put your open hands in front of both ears, with the palms facing forwards. Then sing.

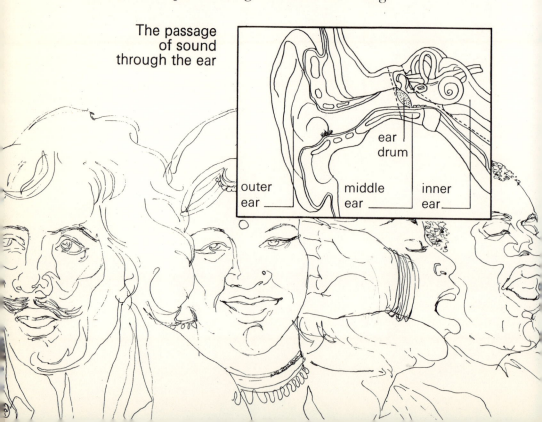

The passage of sound through the ear

ear drum

outer ear   middle ear   inner ear

Singing Teachers

You can now appreciate why a singing teacher has always had a close relationship with his pupil, who cannot see his instrument, watch his diaphragm, or tune his larynx. He has to rely on the methods of breathing and practice suggested by his teacher, and notice, when praised, how it feels in his own body to produce "good" notes.

A sensitive ear will help a singer to distinguish small differences between sounds. Many teachers recommend playing an instrument such as the violin, so that the student can learn, by making and playing notes, to listen to the pitch, and so improve his own sense of singing in tune, or intonation. Also, although a teacher will give his pupil guidance on interpreting a song—that is, putting it across to an audience—many singers find it invaluable to learn the piano, to read accompaniments, and be able to study a song fully as it is prepared for performance.

There have been countless teaching theories and fashions. Different kinds of voices have been popular at different times, and composers' use of the human voice has called for different styles of singing through the centuries. You can demonstrate this for yourself by comparing the sort of voice admired not so long ago in the earliest days of recording: Dame Nellie Melba first in 1902, and Caruso in 1905, with Birgit Nilsson and Dietrich Fischer-Dieskau singing today with markedly different voice production. Differing voice production techniques have developed in various countries. The English version is now a blend of the German and Italian.

Early vocal composers like Palestrina (1525-94), Monteverdi (1567-1643), and sometimes Bach (1685-1750), tended to use the voice as an instrument, the most expressive one of all. An intriguing modern treatment of the voice by the Swingle Singers has employed voices as wind instruments, singing the parts of Bach's music wordlessly. In his day, and earlier, beautiful tone and excellent control were the first aims. *Bel canto* or "beautiful song" was the admiring term given to the great seventeenth- and eighteenth-century singers. Italians were admired most. More dramatic use of the voice was demanded in early operas and oratorios when the voice adopted a declaiming style.

Then the voice had to "act" more in such operas as Mozart's

(1756–91), become more dramatic and powerful in operas by Verdi (1813–1901) and Wagner (1813–83), more personally involved and emotional in the songs of Schubert (1797–1828) and Richard Strauss (1864–1949).

Perhaps the human voice is as adaptable to fashion as a woman's shape is said to be, as she has shaped it to curve out from corsets or be trim in trousers.

The Italian Farinelli, singing in London in 1737, was applauded for five minutes after just one note, in which he displayed his power to increase and decrease his volume. Other singers were pelted with rotten oranges, or sonnets written to praise them. Applause might be banging with sticks, or, in church, coughing and nose-blowing. In Dublin, in 1831, a singer was made to *stand* on the piano, to be seen better by the audience.

So when we hear of riotous fans mobbing singers today, we can say that opera-goers behaved with similar enthusiasm long ago. There is a power in the human voice to excite an audience, whether it is by the beauty of the music, the drama and poetry of the words, or a musicianly combination of both. A good singer reaches his audience, and touches them with his persuasive art.

The eighteenth-century
singer Farinelli
in a woman's role

Types of Singer

Voices are divided into four main groups, according to the compass, or range of notes from low to high, which can be sung with ease.

The *soprano* is the high female voice with a compass reaching from about middle C to the C two octaves above.

The *mezzo-soprano* is a slightly lower voice, the most common one.

The *contralto* has a range starting with the G below middle C, upwards for less than two octaves. It is a deep voice, rich in tone.

A boy's high voice before it breaks is called a *treble*. If his voice remains high, it is called a *tenor*, and his compass will start from the C below middle C, upwards for nearly two octaves.

Another male voice is the *counter-tenor*, with a range a fifth higher than the tenor's. (The interval a "fifth" is five letter names, as C to G on the piano.) This male soprano is a singer who has concentrated on the highest notes he can reach to the extent that they are as well produced as the more conventional range of adult male singers.

The *baritone* is the flexible male voice with a medium range. The *bass* is the deepest voice, and some singers can reach even two and a half octaves below middle C. Try out the notes on a piano.

MUSIC FOR SINGING

The singer has an immense repertoire, ranging from old folk songs and hymn tunes to the complicated, "advanced" writing of some composers today, who again, as if the voice were an ordinary wind instrument, expect the singer to perform great feats of agility. The voice is "stretched" by new demands to leap from note to note, producing different textures of tone, almost shrieks, but whispers too. Listen to a piece by Berio, Boulez or Stockhausen to hear how the traditional demands for singing clear tunes have been changed. Singers who have "absolute pitch", knowing which note is which instinctively rather than by training, are in a strong position to sing in competition with electronic music and instruments playing in experimental fashion and rhythms.

Many teachers recommend singing in choirs, at least in early stages, so that a singer learns to listen to other voices, and discipline his own to blend with them.

The solo singer then is ready to form an equal partnership with his accompanist. If you listen to Gerald Moore accompanying on the piano, and read what he has written about his work, you will realize that the pianist by no means just follows. He supports the singer musically.

Song is a balanced work of art, presenting poetry with music. Neither "wins": each should complement the other. The singer's aim is to convey to an audience what the composer and poet had in mind. That is interpretation.

Lute Songs

In Europe a peak of excellence was reached by lute songs during the sixteenth century. The lute accompanied verses of a high standard, poetry fit to stand alone, but its beauty enhanced by the ayres such composers as John Dowland (c.1563–1626) set to it. Sometimes extra parts were written for other voices to join in.

The German Lied (Song)

Early in the nineteenth century, a movement in art, literature and music gathered force. It was called the Romantic Movement, and gave more weight to subject matter, to personal feelings, than to the shape or form of music. The song, as a blend of poetry and music, blossomed. Composers found their inspiration in the Romantic poetry of Scott and Goethe, and in the well developed

Playing the lute

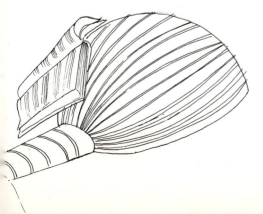

piano, which could match the singer's expressive voice.

Schubert wrote over six hundred songs, in which the accompaniment is inseparably linked with the words, so perfectly does one set off the other. Listen to Benjamin Britten and Peter Pears performing the terrifying story-song, "Der Erlkönig", or the group of songs, the song cycle *Die Schöne Müllerin*.

Schubert was followed by such composers as Schumann (1810–1856), Brahms (1833–97), and Wolf (1860–1903).

In lighter vein, this century there have been Jerome Kern (1885–1945), George Gershwin (1898–1937), many excellent song writers for stage and film musicals, the folk singer Bob Dylan, the Beatles, Lennon and McCartney, and scores of others.

Church Music and Oratorio

Church music has produced its own choristers throughout its long history. During his lifetime, St Philip Neri (1515–95) began to bring into his church services parts of mystery plays set to music. He was hoping to attract young people into his church in Rome, just as today pop groups are sometimes invited to play and perform musicals in cathedrals.

In time, large scale musical settings, usually of sacred words, developed and, from 1600, were called oratorios. The name has been used rather loosely, but can include the famous settings of the story of Jesus' passion by Schütz (1585–1672) and by Bach in his Passions according to St Matthew and St John.

In England, there is a special affection for Handel's *Messiah*, written in 1742, and performed to George II, who stood in admiration for the "Hallelujah Chorus", a custom still observed at the countless performances given annually by choral societies. Haydn's *Creation*, written in 1798, Mendelssohn's *Elijah* in 1846, Elgar's *Dream of Gerontius* in 1900, and Walton's *Belshazzar's Feast* in 1931, may all challenge and absorb you later on, as a choir singer.

Opera

You will probably first approach opera as a listener, on record, or watch performances or extracts on television, unless you join in amateur productions of Gilbert and Sullivan's comic operas, such as *The Pirates of Penzance*.

For opera is a form of music which asks from its singers the ability to sing and to act. The singer has to portray a character as well as to interpret the music. He must convince his audience twice over.

In Italy, late in the sixteenth century, a "new music" was developed, reacting against group choral singing, by setting dialogue naturally as if spoken, in "recitative" for a single voice accompanied by a few chords. This grew into a dramatic representation of a story by sung music. The first opera of this kind was staged in about 1600. One of the first operas, still known and performed today, was Monteverdi's *Orfeo* of 1607. He went on to develop the long solo, which became the *Aria* (air), and gradually, during the eighteenth century, grew into a means of display of brilliant vocal fireworks. Singers were idolized. Technical skill predominated. But opera also attracted composers like the German Gluck (1714–87), who restated the need for acting, clear action and the importance of orchestral support. Mozart followed, and sometimes introduced spoken dialogue into his superb operas, where the music itself describes the characters.

Verdi and Puccini (1858–1924) continued the "grand" and melodramatic Italian tradition in such works as *Aïda* and *Madame Butterfly*. Wagner composed giant music dramas with heroic voices floating over waves of orchestral sound. Today, Britten (born 1913) has written operas, some for children, which bring new life to the elaborate and exotic entertainment which yokes music with drama in one magnificent whole. There are so many operas to see and hear. Records as well can introduce you to an overpowering experience.

It is not surprising that the word "enchant" is related to the Latin word meaning "to sing", because the human voice can enthrall us. The greatest conductors of orchestras are often most praised because they teach the players to "sing" with their various instruments. How they achieve this miracle, a "choir" of hundreds of different voices, is the subject of the next section, musical instruments.

2　The Instruments of Music

AN INSTRUMENT IS a contrivance which makes a musical sound.
Or perhaps we should say it is a contrivance which can make a
musical sound, because a violin can screech, a trumpet wail, a
drum rasp, almost deafen.

What makes their sound musical is a correct and skilled use of
the instruments by a player. An instrument is just a lifeless article
of wood, metal or other fabric until the player makes it speak with
its own distinctive voice. In a way, even that is too simple, because
some people would argue about what a musical sound is. They
would, for instance, like to dismiss many modern experiments
with electronic instruments as the production of hideous din,
nothing to do with the beauty of music.

So what we can safely say is that we look to musical instruments
to provide us with patterns of sound which can express, in a form
no other art can, something satisfying and agreeable to our ears.

The range of musical instruments is vast. An instrument can be
small enough to cup in one hand, like a little mouth organ or
harmonica, or it can be a giant organ, with hundreds of pipes,
whose sounds can fill a hall holding thousands of people.

There are old instruments, lovingly restored or copied by today's
craftsmen; there are new inventions, powered by electricity. We
can only outline a path through them all. Then you can find out
much more for yourself. You can listen hard to music, and try and
decide which instrument is playing. Benjamin Britten's *Young
Person's Guide to the Orchestra: Variations and Fugue on a Theme of*

Church organ | Mouth organ
Ship's bell　Hand bell

Purcell, demonstrating by a set of variations the different sounds, is an excellent introduction.

Also you can look out for instruments in junk shops and other people's homes. Museums often have instruments in their collections. The Victoria and Albert Museum in London has an enterprising sort of juke-box, on which you can hear recordings of some of its old instruments. Recitals are given on their instruments at times as well. If an instrument in playing order is not too fragile, you just might even be allowed to touch and play it. Private collectors are often willing to play and show how their instruments work.

What was the first musical sound you heard in your life, apart from singing? It might have been recorded music, from radio, television or record player. Or it might have been a door bell. Now if your door had a ringing or chiming bell, that was a musical sound. If it had a buzzer, then you heard a noise. There is the distinction and the difference, clear to you in your cradle!

A bell is a simple instrument: a hollow cup shape of metal, which rings when it is tapped by a hammer, or clapper hung within. Yet there is great variety. A bell can dangle to tinkle from a finger, or be so huge that it needs cranes to lift it to swing in a church tower, weighing tons. One in St Paul's Cathedral weighs nearly seventeen tons.

We divide up musical instruments into groups, according to the way that the musical sound is made, and they can be arranged like this: percussion instruments; keyboard instruments; stringed instruments; wind instruments: woodwind and brass; electronic instruments; mechanical instruments. In the following chapters you can read about some of the instruments in all these categories and look at diagrams (not necessarily drawn to scale).

MUSICAL PERFORMANCE

It is not only in space that men are crossing new frontiers. Instrumentalists today are looking abroad to the exotic instruments of faraway countries such as India. They are looking into the past, rediscovering forgotten old instruments, restoring them and copying them. Then, as they study the scores which were written for old instruments, they want to play exactly what the original composer heard, perhaps centuries ago. It is not uncommon to

The instruments of a modern orchestra.
The numbers vary
for different performances.

1 double bass
2 first and second
   violins
3 horns
4 clarinets
5 bass clarinet
6 piccolo
7 flutes
8 cor anglais
9 timpani
10 bass and side drum
11 xylophone

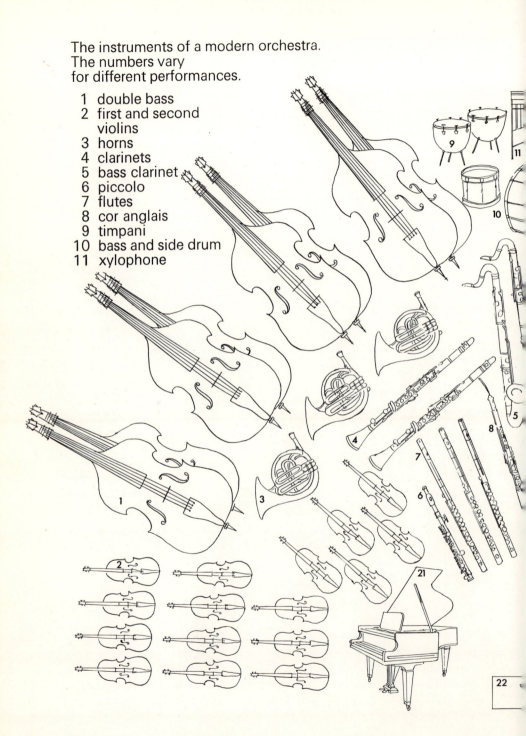

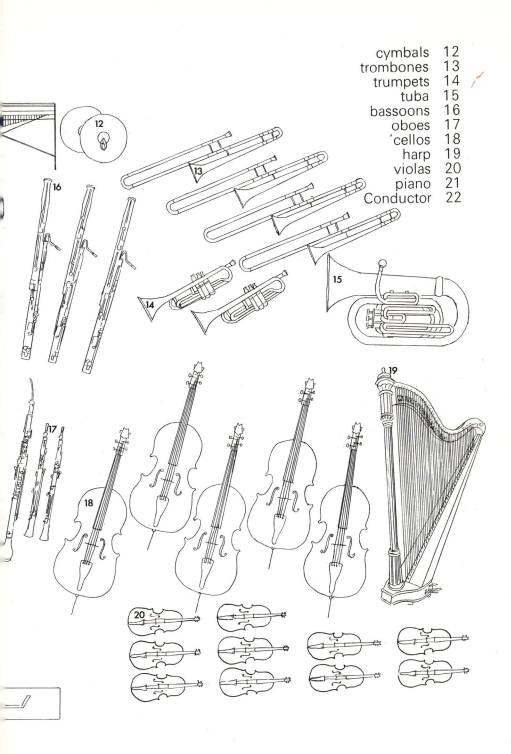

hear groups specially formed to play medieval music on, for instance, shawms, psalteries, organs and lutes. A recently founded orchestra has been modelled on the French King Louis XIV's *Vingt-Quatre Violons du Roi*, using stringed instruments and bows of this period (1638–1715), and so producing new sounds for modern ears.

Most large towns and cities have visits from symphony orchestras, so you can hear large scale works performed live, as well as on records; and you can study how a conductor contrives to draw from so many players his own personal interpretation of what the composer wished to be heard. You can watch players in concert halls and on television to see how they use their instruments, and what they sound like. Some conductors use batons or sticks, others just their hands: of course, they do far more than beat time.

Pages 26–27 show an arrangement of the seating of a symphony orchestra, but a conductor may change it for his own reasons, or to

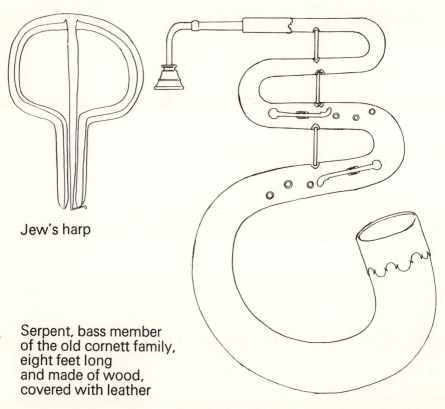

Jew's harp

Serpent, bass member
of the old cornett family,
eight feet long
and made of wood,
covered with leather

suit the demands of a particular score.

Often today, instead of being conducted in the modern manner, groups are "led" in the old style by the harpsichordist, or the first violin, or a soloist. Orchestras and ensembles are not invariably rigid groups, because this is also an age of experiment. A composer may call upon players from a pool of instrumentalists, and then combine their playing with sounds from a battery of tape-recorders.

The Swiss oboist and composer, Heinz Holliger, has described another development which is taking place. As a characteristic contemporary composer, he is seeking new sounds. Applying this to his own instrument, he is making use of all the sounds he can produce. And it is an amazing range. He breathes in and out of his oboe. He tries different "attacks" to sound notes, clicking with his tongue or his throat. He uses his tongue as a percussion instrument touching the oboe's reed. He can make the harmonics or overtones sound out. And if he uses a trumpet embouchure, he can sound different tones from the oboe's usual voice, tones you might not at first recognize.

Perhaps within other musical instruments there are potentialities still to be discovered, even by those players who, like Holliger, can play the "classical" music of Mozart superbly, with the accepted, traditional sounds, as well as exploratory pieces.

You may never become a virtuoso player. Yet you can gain enormous pleasure from association with a musical instrument of some kind. You can simply make your own comb music, blowing tunes through greaseproof paper folded over a comb. Or you can improvise your own percussion instrument with spoons, waste metal and twanging bands. You can discover for yourself how a Jew's harp can be made to sound in your mouth. Or whether you can blow a note on an old serpent. It's not easy.

You can try to rig up your version of a piano without a frame, whose strings are merely attached to the wall of your house. (That was thought of in 1854.)

Yet whatever you play, or try to play, you are never quite alone with a musical instrument. Another voice can speak to you, answer you, echo what you sing, express what you are feeling or thinking. With its help you can create afresh music which conveys what no words can say.

3 Percussion Instruments

As a baby, you may have had a rattle to shake or a toy drum to beat. At some stage you probably banged your high chair or cot with a wooden spoon. If so, you improvised a percussion instrument, which means that you made a sound by striking one object against another.

At school, you may have played in a percussion or rhythm band, keeping time to a lead from the teacher at the piano.

Your band would sound well because the teacher not only gave the beat, but also the tune. For all these instruments have no exact pitch; that is, they cannot make differing high or low notes. They cannot even play "Baa baa black sheep". But, because they emphasize the rhythm so attractively with the extra colour of their sounds, we take them to be musical sound makers, though really they make "noise".

To accompany dancing, when it is particularly important to hear the beat of the music, many percussion instruments are used. Even a typewriter once was played for its clickety-clack in a piece by a Frenchman, Erik Satie.

Children playing
percussion instruments

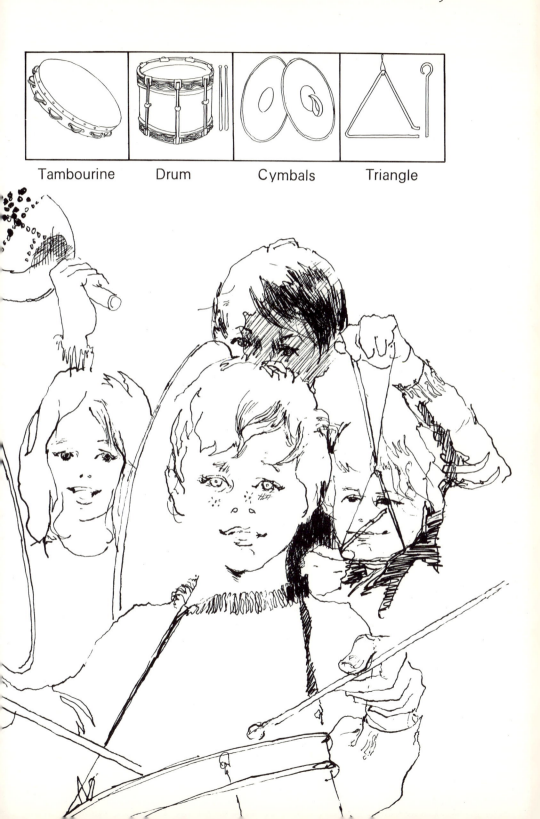

Tambourine   Drum   Cymbals   Triangle

THE PERCUSSION BAND

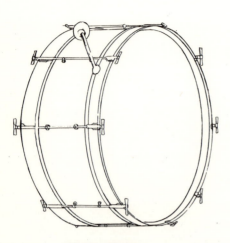

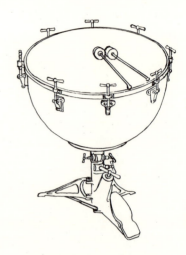

Bass drum   Kettle drum or timpani

Drums

Drums include instruments of no definite pitch, which just boom or roll, and kettledrums or timpani which can be tuned to sound notes. In a big orchestra, a player may have three or more drums, which he tunes by tightening the head or lid of calf skin or vellum or plastic with screws. The smaller and tighter the drum, the higher the note it sounds when, to get the clearest sound, he beats between the edge and the centre.

Cymbals

Made of brass, with leather handles, they are clashed together. To stop them vibrating and ringing, the player rests them on his body.

Tambourine

The tambourine is a hoop of wood, covered with parchment; the metal discs threaded in its side are called jingles, and ring when the tambourine is shaken, or tapped with the fingers.

Triangle

The bent steel rod is struck with the beater, and sounds a note if it is swinging free, to vibrate. If the stick is moved from side to side, the triangle tinkles.

TUNED PERCUSSION INSTRUMENTS

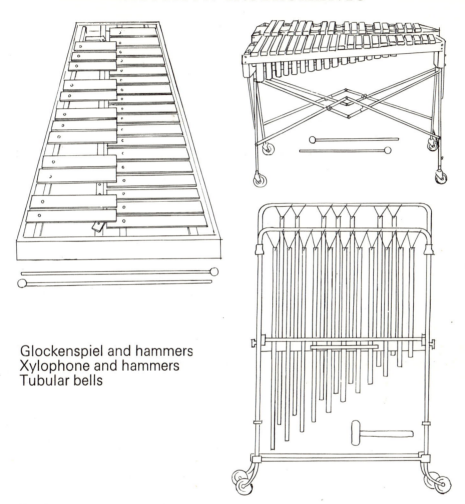

Glockenspiel and hammers
Xylophone and hammers
Tubular bells

In the nineteen-twenties, a German called Carl Orff decided that the best way for young children to learn about music was to beat its rhythms. He introduced what he called melodic percussion, adding simple tuned instruments, so that children could not only sing the tune with the teacher's piano lead, but play some of the notes too.

Chime Bars and Glockenspiel

You may have used or seen chime bars or glockenspiels. Chime bars are strips of metal pinned over a hollow metal block, which sound a note when struck with a hammer. Glockenspiels have two rows of graduated steel bars, again fastened across a hollow wooden frame, so that they vibrate and sound when they are tapped with wooden rubber-tipped beaters. The sound is bell-like, as the name meaning "bell-play" suggests. In military bands, glockenspiels are sometimes carried upright, set in curved frames, and the tinkling sound is a striking contrast with the brass voice and drum booms.

Xylophone

The xylophone is played in the same way. Its bars are made of wood, and in modern instruments they are made to resound by metal tubes hung below them as resonators.

Vibraphone

The vibraphone was designed in America, in the nineteen-twenties, and is heard in modern pieces and in pop music today. The metal alloy bars have metal tubes underneath, which are opened and shut by clockwork or electrically powered fans. These can make the sound waver in a *vibrato* long after the bar has been struck.

Chimes

Chimes make bell sounds by long metal tubes hung in a wooden frame being tapped by a rawhide hammer, at the top.

The percussion section of an orchestra is sometimes nicknamed "the kitchen", because of the banging and rattling which takes place there. A great assortment of "effects" is now called for by composers: cowbells, metal chains, an anvil, a whip, a thundersheet, wood blocks to clash together, all these and many more may be found. Many schools, making their own music, have experimented with the sounds they can produce from tapping suspended brake discs, bottles, cups, earthenware flower pots, saucepan lids, biscuit tin drums.

You can experiment too, for intriguing sounds can be conjured from the most simple materials if you start tapping with wooden spoons or thimbled fingers, and allow the tapped object to vibrate so that its voice can be heard.

4 Keyboard Instruments

Piano and Clavichord

It is very likely that you hear a piano played every school day, and are familiar with its sound and appearance. You could ask to have the front wooden panel lifted off so that you could look at the "works" inside. See how the notes are made.

In essence, the piano is a percussion instrument, because the sound is produced by striking one object against another. In this case, the strings are tapped by felt-tipped wooden hammers. The

Upright piano with front panel removed

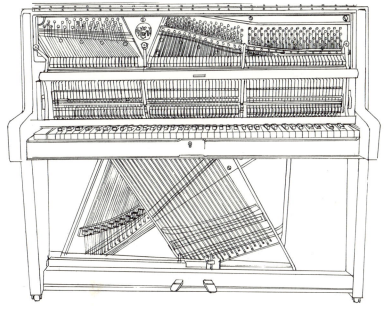

Interior of clavichord

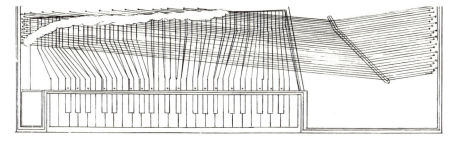

advantage of a keyboard instrument is that one player's two hands can control a large number of hammers at once. If you are a player, you will know that it is your fingerwork, your ability to move your fingers and thumbs independently one from the other, which makes you able to use the keyboard well.

The direct ancestor of our piano is the clavichord, which was popular from at least the fourteenth to the late eighteenth century.

The clavichord's strings are struck by tangents, which are wedge-shaped blades of brass set upright at the end of each key. When the key is pressed down, the tangent rises to tap the string and stays touching it until the key is released. Because of this action, a slight extra pressure of the finger on a key can increase tension on the string and raise the pitch of the note's sound. Finger play on the keys can control loud and soft and a gentle repeating of the note, called *Bebung*. Because of its expressiveness, it was often used for teaching singing, and was popular for practising by organists.

The clavichord was gradually ousted by the new pianoforte. Though there were earlier experiments, an Italian, Cristofori, is given the credit for inventing a keyboard instrument *col piano e forte*, "with soft and loud", in Florence in 1709.

One difference from the clavichord and earlier instruments is

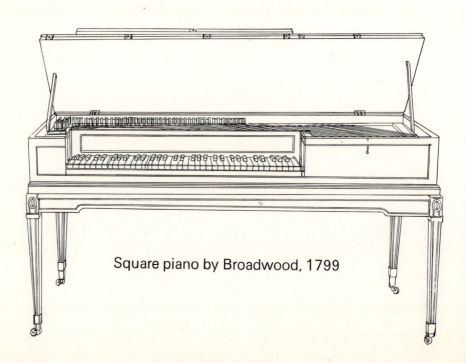

Square piano by Broadwood, 1799

that the pianoforte's fingers do not directly "play" the string with the key. Try for yourself. If you press a piano key very gently, no sound is heard. You have to press it firmly enough for the hammers to be lifted to the strings by pieces of wood called hoppers, or jacks. When the key is pressed, the jack strikes the hammer which rises to hit the string. A device lets the hammer fall back from the strings, leaving them vibrating. Dampers are raised when the key is pressed down, and fall back when the key is released, stopping the sound.

There have been many experiments and refinements since the first pianos enabled pianists to play loudly and softly and smoothly at will. In England, they were at first called fortepianos. Early square pianos, actually oblong in shape, were made in England by Zumpe, then Broadwood (still making pianos today), from about 1760.

Bach's son, Johann Christian Bach (1735–82), known as the English Bach because of his long residence in England, was a skilful pianist and composer for the instrument, which he championed and helped to make popular.

But it was Mozart who really developed for the piano a style of

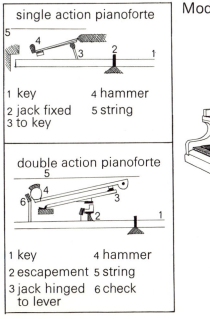

single action pianoforte

1 key   4 hammer
2 jack fixed   5 string
3 to key

double action pianoforte

1 key   4 hammer
2 escapement   5 string
3 jack hinged 6 check
  to lever

Modern baby grand piano

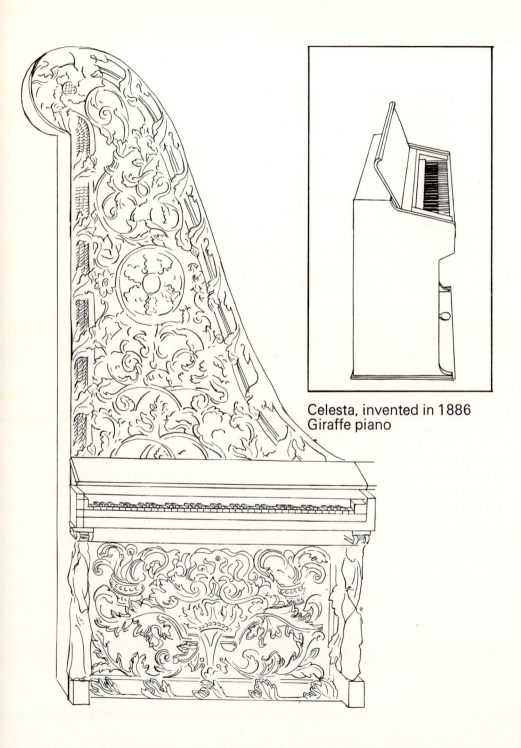

Celesta, invented in 1886
Giraffe piano

music which was its own, triumphantly and distinctively. In 1777, he wrote to his father, praising Stein's pianofortes:

"When I strike hard I can leave my finger on the key, but on taking it away the sound dies away almost immediately. I can do with the keys what I like; the tone is always equal; it does not tinkle disagreeably; it has neither the fault of being too loud nor too soft, nor does it fail entirely. In a word, the tone is perfectly equal throughout. . . ."

Mozart wrote to celebrate this solo instrument more than twenty piano concertos, including one for three pianos, and many sonatas. The developments of the instrument to the one we know today were all concerned with improving the key's action, and the resulting tone. This meant strengthening the instrument's frame, so that strings could be stronger and stretched more tightly. The frames of square pianos could be distorted if the strings were stressed too much. Experiments were made with upright pianos from about the middle of the eighteenth century. First of all, in "Giraffe" pianos, the strings were stretched up from the keyboard. Then the long bass strings were crossed over, or "overstrung" to allow for extra length and the upright shape we know today established. Early in the nineteenth century, iron was used in piano frameworks and Broadwood displayed one in London at the Great Exhibition of 1851. This meant that strings could be stretched at great tension, without the risk of splitting wood; and you can see today a "concert grand" piano, eight feet nine inches in length, with very considerable weight of down-tension on the sound board.

By contrast, minipianos are also made for small rooms, and the celesta (usually grouped with the percussion in an orchestra) is a little keyboard instrument, whose hammers strike steel plates attached to wooden resonators.

The development of the pianoforte has been matched by an enormous wealth of music. Many great composers have started as pianists, have "conducted" from the instrument, and have drafted their works at the keyboard. After Mozart, Beethoven, writing his first piano concerto in 1795, made testing demands on the instrument to produce dramatic effects. Liszt (1811–86) encouraged pupils to sit higher from the piano so that they could bring more

Liszt at the piano

force to the weight of their hands. He often spoke of hurting the piano with his hands, and even broke hammers and strings in intensely emotional performances. Chopin (1810–49) preferred to develop a gentle touch that would produce a singing and sustained line of melody.

Harpsichord, Virginals and Spinet

Perhaps the most interesting thing today about the "early" keyboard instruments, the harpsichord, virginals and spinet, is that they are no longer early, but contemporary as well. For during this century, and earlier, there has been a revival of interest in playing older music as the composer himself would have heard it. This led such pioneers as Arnold Dolmetsch (1858–1940) back to the study, and then to the reproduction of old instruments. His father, a piano maker, learnt from his father who was an organ builder. Arnold Dolmetsch learnt to play the clavichord, and, in Haslemere, Surrey, began to make again clavichords, harpsichords, spinets and virginals. These last three are really versions of one keyboard instrument, in which the horizontal strings are plucked. When the finger key is pressed down a jack, holding a quill or point of leather, rises and plucks the string as it passes. Then it falls without touching the string again, by means of an escapement mechanism.

These instruments were popular from early in the sixteenth to

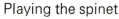
Playing the spinet

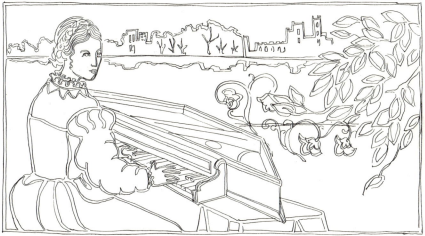

the end of the eighteenth century. The virginals was the simplest, usually in an oblong box, often placed on a table, but sometimes mounted on a four-legged frame. The spinet was usually wing-shaped, and nicknamed the "couched harp" or "triangle virginals". The cases were often elaborately decorated and inlaid, and the Victoria and Albert Museum in London has a hexagonal spinet on which are emblazoned the arms of Queen Elizabeth I, to whom it probably belonged.

The harpsichord was the largest of the three, and produced the

Above : Interior of virginals Below : Joseph Haydn's harpsichord, with two   anuals

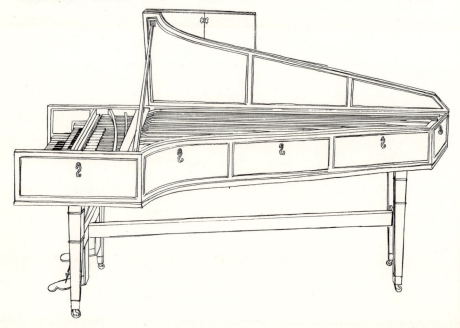

greatest tone, sometimes having two, three, or four sets of strings, sounding an octave above or below and controlled by stops. You will recognize its sound as a "twang", which does not reverberate for long. Some had two keyboards.

Throughout the seventeenth and eighteenth centuries, this instrument was used to support groups and orchestras, and sometimes a composer directed his work from the keyboard, not "conducting" as we would expect today. The early piano, with its superior powers of tone and sustaining sound, banished the harpsichords to attics and scrap heaps, until they were rescued and brought to new life again.

Arnold Dolmetsch built his first harpsichord in 1896. Today there are several firms who specialize in making "early" keyboard instruments. Although they can and do experiment with new materials, there is no substitute for the laborious handwork of craftsmen in assembling and adjusting the instruments, which are therefore costly. But musicians take great pleasure in producing authentic music, true to its time. The movement is gathering momentum. So, as well as harpsichords playing Bach's music, you may hear recordings of Beethoven's played on the sort of pianoforte which was available to him, early in the nineteenth century. You will be able to distinguish a fruity, ringing tone, quite different from a modern instrument.

Layout of the pipes
of the Festival Hall organ, London

The Organ

A modern organ is the largest and most complicated instrument which one person can play, using his hands to manipulate two, three or four keyboards, or manuals, and at the same time change stops, which vary the tone, while his feet press a pedal keyboard also sounding notes. It is hard work.

As well as in churches, you may see an organ in a concert hall, its ranks of pipes well in view. There may be thousands of pipes, hundreds of stops, but in essence the organ is a box of whistles, made to sound by bellows. The stops control which set of pipes is being used, and each keyboard works many sets of pipes. The varied size of the pipes can produce notes which sound like other wind instruments, such as the flute, oboe, bassoon and trumpet.

It is interesting to notice that many organists prefer to play the music of Bach and his contemporaries on the sort of small chamber organ he played, which had a very clear bright tone; many

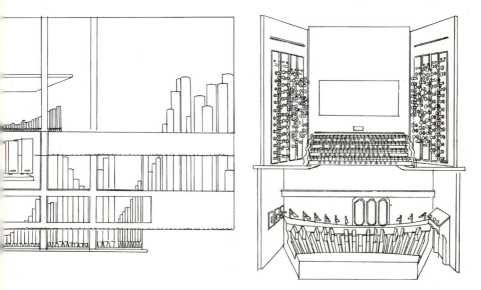

A modern organ keyboard

eighteenth-century church organs survive in Germany and Holland today. Players choose this piercing timbre rather than the giant tones possible from a modern instrument for which the wind is obtained by an electrically driven fan.

Harmonium

Based on the principle of the Chinese mouth organ, or sheng, this keyboard instrument is a free reed organ. Metal reeds are vibrated, blown by two foot pedals, worked alternately. It was and still is used in small chapels or churches, which do not own an organ.

The rather wailing droning sound it produces has attracted pop musicians, and Indian musicians have also adopted it sometimes, combining this or the piano accordion with their own native instruments.

5 Stringed Instruments

Guitarist

THE STRINGS OF all stringed instruments "speak" or sound when they are made to vibrate, by being struck, plucked or rubbed. The note the string sounds will depend on how long it is (the longer the string the deeper the note), how thick, and how tightly stretched. The sound will be amplified if the strings are within or attached to a resonator, such as the body of a violin.

FRETTED INSTRUMENTS

It is likely that the stringed instrument which you know best by sight and sound is the guitar. This instrument has gut frets tied round its fingerboard to mark it out. It is enormously popular, and the passion for it is common to those who enjoy early and classical music and those who prefer progressive pop. Folk singers and jazz players also find it indispensable for their music.

In fact, today the guitar is really a family of three main instruments, related but capable of producing very different sounds, and therefore suitable for different styles of music.

Classical or Spanish Guitar

This guitar is played with the thumb, fingers and fingernails of the right hand. The left hand presses down the string on to the fingerboard; this determines the length that vibrates, and thus the pitch of the note that sounds. The frets or marking bands on the fingerboard make the division of the strings an easier task.

Learning the correct technique is extremely important in playing this instrument, and also an ability to read music, or guitar notation, for learning is done by graded exercises, leading to a wealth of music. Segovia (born 1890) and now younger players, like Julian Bream and John Williams, play not only Spanish music, but arrangements of lute music, and works by Bach, Scarlatti, Haydn and Mendelssohn. A slightly lighter instrument is used in Spain to accompany the traditional "flamenco" singing and dancing.

Flat-Top or Folk Guitar

This instrument is often nicknamed a jumbo guitar, because usually its body is large, and its neck long and narrow. The classical guitar has nylon strings (the three bass ones wound round with wire), whereas the jumbo's strings are of steel (some wrapped with nylon). They give a less soft, a brighter tone, which you can distinguish. The guitar has to have a steel rod within to strengthen it against the strong pull of the strings. And the wear and tear on finger tips is considerable, though they do harden up. Some players use a plastic plectrum or fingerpick, or finger pieces fitted on to their nails when plucking the strings.

The essence of folk guitar playing is the development of your own style. You learn a basic technique, then you improvise from that, using your instrument to create the sounds and patterns you want to make. You will work out your own versions of songs and tunes, each time creating something individual and new.

Ideally, the music is passed on by hearing and by watching. Many players have spent hours watching the blind American masters, like Doc Watson, to find out exactly how, with unerring touch, they made their guitars plink, sing, wail, strum, throb, bring to life the music they meant to hear.

Classical or Spanish guitar   Flat-top or Folk guitar

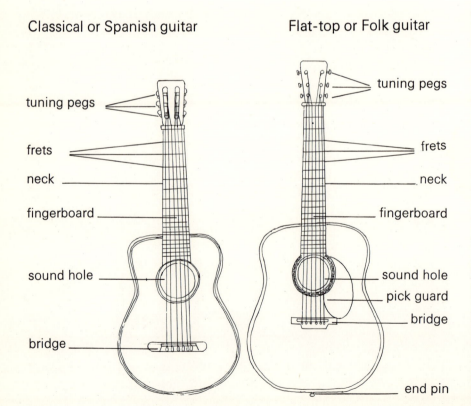

tuning pegs

frets

neck

fingerboard

sound hole

bridge

tuning pegs

frets

neck

fingerboard

sound hole

pick guard

bridge

end pin

Dance-Band Guitar

The sound that this kind of guitar makes with its steel strings is often amplified electrically. Then it can hold its own with the other, louder instruments in a jazz or rock group. Either the actual sounds from the guitar itself are amplified, or the instrument is modified again, into a skeleton guitar. From this the strings' actual vibrations are converted into electrical impulses, and the resulting sounds are familiar from the work of scores of pop groups.

The exciting quality of the guitar is its versatility. A first instrument can be comparatively cheap. A player can carry looped on his back the means to murmur a piece by the Spanish composer Albéniz, to accompany his own version of *Saint James' Infirmary Blues*, or to belt out with others a rock number to make the floor boards shudder and the ceiling shake. It is the instrument of modern minstrels.

You can best see how it is done by watching close-ups on films and television. And to taste the multifarious styles, and choose your favourites, there are countless records.

Dance-band guitar

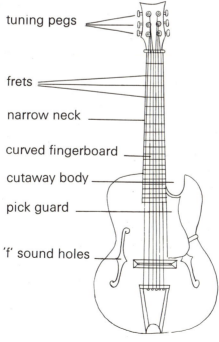

tuning pegs

frets

narrow neck

curved fingerboard

cutaway body

pick guard

'f' sound holes

Lute   Mandoline

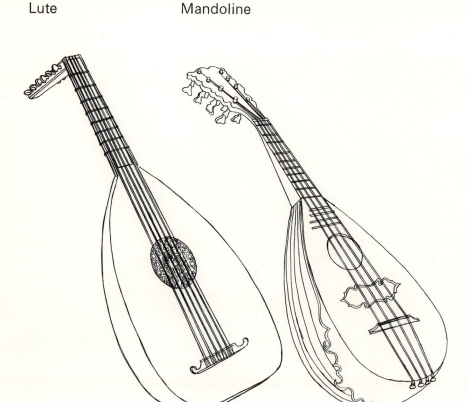

Lute

The lute is an early fretted instrument, less robust than the guitar; a good lute's body is so delicate that it can tremble in the hand in response to sounds near it, as small as a speaking voice. Old instruments and copies are used to play early music today.

Mandoline

Developed from an Italian form of lute, the mandoline has an echoing tone, and has been used for this quality by Mozart, Handel, Beethoven, Mahler and Stravinsky.

Zither

This is a popular folk instrument in South Germany and Austria. Some strings, for the melody, are fastened over a fretted finger-

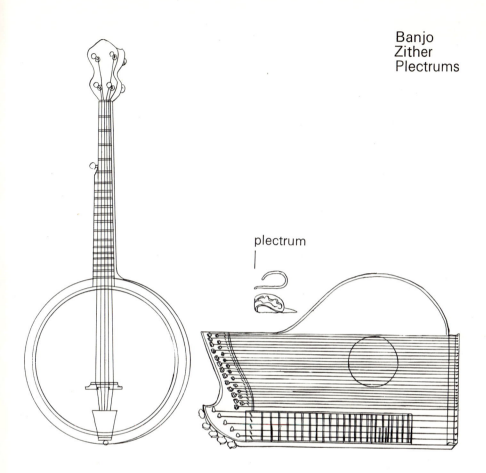

plectrum

board, fingered by the left hand and plucked with a plectrum worn on the right thumb. The fingers of the right hand play the other strings, as the instrument lies flat on knees or a table.

Banjo

This started life as a Negro instrument, often playing with a fiddle. At first, its belly was of vellum stretched over a wooden hoop. Many varieties were made and played by amateurs, by music hall singers, such as George Formby, in jazz bands, and in string bands with mandolines and guitars. It has a distinct harsh twang, which some groups have brought into favour again, to contrast its tone with guitars. In America it is heard in bluegrass and country music.

THE VIOLIN FAMILY

The four members of this group of instruments speak with voices that blend together well. Their stretched strings are made to vibrate by the friction of a bow, and to reverberate through the instrument's body. Two violins, a viola and 'cello make up a string quartet, the most popular group for chamber music. Then double-basses join the three to form the string section in an orchestra.

An artist's impression of the 'cellist Paul Tortelier

Violin

Various stringed instruments abounded before the sixteenth century, but the violin family we know today was brought to perfection by a group of Italians living in Cremona from the mid-sixteenth to the early eighteenth century. Among these the most famous was Antonio Stradivari (c.1644–1737). His "Strad" violins are now worth huge sums of money, because of their superlative tone. The Amati and Guarneri families also produced instruments whose quality has delighted and mystified violin makers ever since.

The violin appears to be a simple, hollow, decorated box, about fourteen inches long, but in fact it has over seventy parts, in various woods, assembled by hand. There is a small wooden cylinder, the bass bar, set within to keep the belly firm against the pull of the strings, and this the Germans nickname the "voice" and the French the "soul" of the violin. In fact, each tiny part can affect the quality of sound. There have been many attempts to rediscover the exact varnish with which Cremona violins were painted, for even this protective layer on the body can change the tone completely, muffling or enhancing it.

The substance of the strings is equally crucial. Cremona violins had gut from young lambs' intestines soaked in alkaline water before being dried and twisted. Today, many varieties are used, such as cores of gut, nylon, steel wire or plastic wound with silver, or stainless steel.

As with a guitar, only without the help of frets, a violinist has to find his own notes on the fingerboard with his left fingers pressing down the strings, altering their "speaking" length. His right hand with curved thumb holds the bow to press it on the strings without scraping. There are various strokes to learn, and sometimes he will pluck the strings with his fingers, *pizzicato*, or tap them with the bow stick, *col legno*.

Starting by tuning his four strings, tightening them with pegs, the violinist has to develop a keen ear, to criticize and correct the sound he creates. Progress may seem slow to a learner, but he is rewarded by producing perhaps the most expressive and eloquent voice of all. The leader of an orchestra is traditionally a violinist; the violins are divided into first and second violins, who may have separate parts to play. Modern modifications have produced a violin with brilliant and flexible tone, audible above a large orchestra. To hear a little of what it can achieve, listen to Mozart's Fifth Violin Concerto, the "Turkish" in A (K 219), written at the astonishing age of nineteen, in 1775, and Mendelssohn's popular Violin Concerto in E minor.

Viola

The viola is a larger instrument, tuned a fifth lower and giving a richer, less piercing sound. So many more solo works have been inspired by the violin, it has tended to overshadow its subtle relation. Yet the viola has a distinct quality, which you can judge for yourself if you listen to the beautiful music Berlioz gave it in *Harold in Italy*, in 1834. Also try and pick it out in string quartets and quintets. It is a superb foil for the violin, as Mozart demonstrated in his Sinfonia Concertante (K 364) for Violin and Viola.

'Cello or Violoncello

The player sits down to perform on this instrument, and his left fingers have twice as far to stretch as on the violin. It cannot be as flexible as its smaller relations, but the tone is beautifully

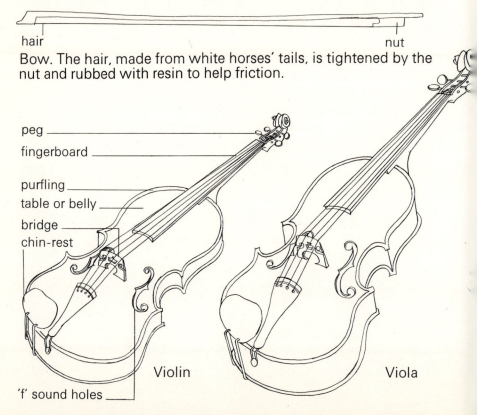

hair   nut

Bow. The hair, made from white horses' tails, is tightened by the nut and rubbed with resin to help friction.

peg

fingerboard

purfling

table or belly

bridge

chin-rest

Violin   Viola

'f' sound holes

mellow, as you can hear in, for example, Elgar's 'Cello Concerto in E minor, written in 1918–19.

Earlier, Haydn had written 'cello concertos; Mendelssohn and Chopin wrote for 'cello and piano, and Brahms' Double Concerto in A for 'cello and violin gives free expression to its rich quality. Richard Strauss made the 'cello take the character of *Don Quix* in the variations he wrote in 1903.

Pablo Casals (1876–1973) developed the technique and artistry of 'cello playing to a peak during this century, and today Rostropovich has a magnificent command of the instrument.

Double Bass

This is over six feet high, and so the player stands, to master this large instrument. Of course, it is not agile but the rich deep tone is indispensable in an orchestra. Also jazz and pop composers have recognized how usefully the instrument's *pizzicato* can strengthen rhythmic impact.

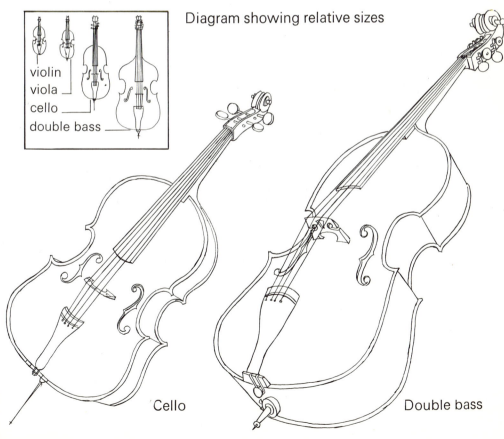

Diagram showing relative sizes

violin
viola
cello
double bass

Cello

Double bass

HARP
There are two main kinds of harp you may see and hear today. One is a Celtic harp, representing a long tradition of folk playing in Ireland, Scotland and Wales, and you can be reminded of this by the common surname, Harper. The revival of interest in older music is prompting players to sing again the Irish songs, accompanying themselves on the harp, plucking at the brass strings which give a penetrating tone, in the old style, with finger nails grown specially long.

Old Welsh harps tended to be tall, and to have horse-hair or gut strings. Today Welsh harpers often use a modern pedal harp for their playing. In the earlier harps, each string produced one note

Irish harp, 1819
Right: Modern pedal harp.
Some strings are coloured,
to be easily recognised by the player.

in a seven note scale of tones. Two or three banks of strings were fastened in one harp, to produce semi-tones, but these were difficult to play.

After many experiments, a Frenchman, Erard, perfected a double-action "pedal harp" in 1810. There are seven foot pedals, and these can shorten each string in two positions. Other technical improvements followed.

This is the harp you will see in a large symphony orchestra, an accepted member since the days of Berlioz (1803–69). Debussy, Ravel and Britten have all written for this instrument with great sympathy, making use of the reverberating tones of its echoing strings.

Playing the harp.

6 Wind Instruments

THESE INSTRUMENTS ARE divided into two main groups, woodwind (flutes and reed instruments) and brass.

WOODWIND INSTRUMENTS

The "wind" is already in these instruments. What the player does is to make the air inside them vibrate, just as the violinist makes his strings vibrate. The less air he puffs into the wind instrument the better and more flexible tone he can make. The sound is lip controlled, and individual to the player, who "chooses" it by the use of his lips, tongue, teeth, mouth cavity, throat and lungs. Ideally, he hears the note he wants to play first in his head, and then breathes and plays to create it.

Recorder (End-blown Flute)

Many schools use recorders as their first musical instruments, and these wooden or plastic whistles blend together well "in consort". Once again, their popularity is due to a revival of interest in older instruments. Recorders were popular in England from late in the fourteenth century, and in the sixteenth and seventeenth centuries English sets of descant (treble), alto, tenor and bass recorders were famous. Bach and Handel used them in their orchestras, but gradually they were replaced by the transverse flute, which was held sideways. It had more flexible dynamics, that is, ability to play loud and soft.

Arnold Dolmetsch (see also p. 41) revived them, and from late in the nineteen-twenties they have been made again. The recorder is open at each end, but there is a "fipple" or plug to form a whistle mouthpiece. Though no longer the price of the humble tin or penny whistle, recorders are inexpensive, and you could

Piccolo
Recorder

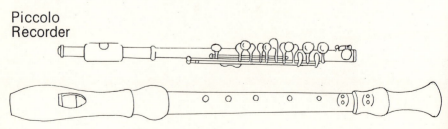

easily buy one and a first instruction book or Method, and experiment yourself. Starting with nursery rhymes, there is a lot you could play.

Sometimes double recorders are made. Panpipes, first played by country shepherds, are folk instruments which survive today as toys. They are a set of tuned tubes joined together and stopped at the bottom, made from bamboo, wood, glass and, today, from plastic.

Another musical toy, still popular as an instrument in Italy, is the ocarina, with nine holes. Bird calls and cuckoo whistles are other globular rather than tube flutes.

A flute can even be blown by the nostrils. The player of a Polynesian nose flute can hum and grunt while he plays; quite a feat.

Panpipes
Nose flute

Transverse or Cross Flutes

A flautist, or flute player, has a choice of a concert flute, whose compass is about three octaves up from middle C, a little piccolo, which sounds an octave higher, an alto, or a bass flute. These two sound a fourth and an octave lower than the concert flute.

The knack of sounding a note with a woodwind instrument is a working relationship between the lips and the tongue. The flute's tube is closed at the head, near which is an elliptical mouth hole. The player blows a tiny airstream *across* the edge of the hole, aiming at the opposite edge. This vibrates the column of air within, and a tone is produced. The pitch of the tone is altered by holes in the flute, covered by finger keys. If a hole is uncovered, it has the effect of shortening the tube: then the note's pitch is raised.

Flutes today are often made in metal, such as silver, rather than in wood.

Bach, Handel, Haydn and Mozart all wrote for the flute, and it is worth looking out for Debussy's attractive short piece for unaccompanied solo flute, *Syrinx*.

Playing a
transverse flute.
From a
seventeenth-century painting

Oboe, Cor Anglais, Bassoon

The upper instruments in this family were called *hautbois*, that is "high wood", which eventually in England became "oboe". This is the treble instrument of the group, like the flute, but it has a reedy, nasal sort of tone. The sound is made by blowing through two delicate reeds, which are bound face to face, then set into a cork base, with a narrow space between. One end of the flexible blades of cane, therefore, can vibrate as the player blows air between, controlling its passage with his lips. Look at a player to see how it is done.

Like the oboe, the cor anglais and bassoon have conical tubes and a double reed. The cor anglais, sounding a fifth lower, has its reed set on a metal tube, curved back for ease of playing.

The bassoon's reed is also set on a curved metal tube. The extra length to produce its bass notes, a twelfth lower than the oboe, is achieved by fashioning it in a U bend. The still deeper contrabassoon is rarely used; its gruff tones are almost comical.

Oboe

Bassoon

Cor Anglais

Oboe reeds, from front and side

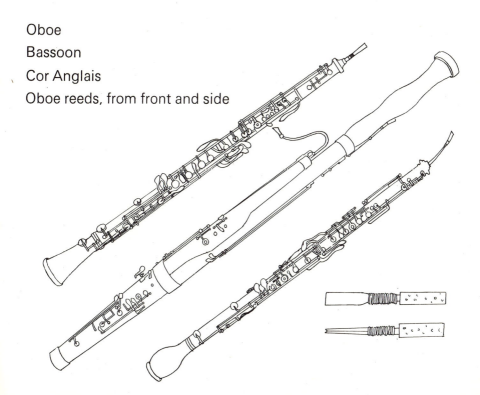

Clarinet

If you listen to Brahms' or Mozart's clarinet quintets, you will be able to recognize the individual tone quality of this instrument. It is perhaps smoother than the other woodwind instruments, yet penetrating.

The clarinet's mouthpiece has a single reed bound to it; this is held against the player's lower lip, curved over his teeth. The tube is cylindrical.

Saxophone

The sound of this instrument will be best known to you from jazz or pop music, although in fact both Vaughan Williams and Benjamin Britten have used it. Sax, who invented it in about 1840, intended to produce a family of instruments for military bands. It is in a way a mongrel, between woodwind and brass, because it has a single reed mouthpiece, like the clarinet, and is conical, but made of brass.

Clarinet and
saxophone players

SOME OTHER WIND INSTRUMENTS

Bagpipes

This ancient instrument still survives today, and Highland pipers gather to play again the *ceòl mór*, the great music of the hereditary master pipers, who used to be attached each to his own clan. They compete in playing the "pibroch", a set of variations.

Usually the bagpipes of Scotland have four reed pipes, a blow pipe, and an airtight leather bag. This bag acts as a bellows, filled with air from the blow pipe, and kept at pressure under the player's arm. Three of the pipes have single reeds and are fixed in pitch. They are called drones, and create the bagpipe's distinctive whine. The fourth pipe has finger holes, to vary the pitch; this "chaunter" plays the tune.

There are also Irish, Breton and Northumbrian versions of the bagpipe, and the Duke of Northumberland still has his own piper.

Bagpipe player

Harmonica or Mouth Organ

This endearing tiny instrument, played cupped in the hand, has been transformed by the playing of Larry Adler: he has tackled many kinds of music, and has even inspired concertos for its reedy voice, one, for example by Vaughan Williams (1872–1958). Look at one, and you will see that metal reeds of varying sizes are fitted into slots in a metal plate, then into a box. Each reed is free to vibrate at one end, and has its own air passage. Notes are made by blowing and sucking in; the expert uses his tongue to cover holes which are not required.

Also jazz and pop groups have adopted it as a distinct voice to contrast with singers. If you listen to the early Beatles' song, "Thank you girl", you will hear the mouth organ wavering over drum beats, and used to point a phrase, sometimes just two or three mouth organ notes giving emphasis.

Concertina

Like the mouth organ, this instrument is a so-called free reed instrument, with metal tongues riveted over a hole for air made in a metal frame. Each reed's pitch depends on its length and thickness: filed at the tip to sharpen or the fixed end to flatten the sounding note. Bellows blow and suck, causing the reed to vibrate to and fro from its sprung-up setting in the frame. Each stud or finger piston controls one note.

Mouth organ or harmonica

Sheng

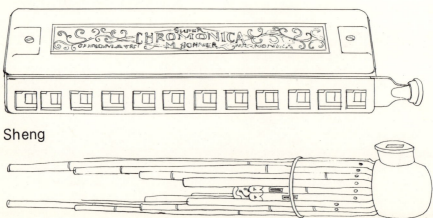

The ancient Chinese mouth organ or "sheng" is really the ancestor of the concertina.

During the late eighteenth century, European musicians became interested in this new sounding instrument, brought from the East. Early in the nineteenth century, various experiments came to fruition with the invention of the concertina. Quartet families of this instrument were made. Tchaikovsky (1840–93) used four in an orchestral suite. There were concertina bands, and the Salvation Army once had one hundred and fifty such groups. Concertinas were extremely popular for light music, until they were ousted by the cheaper piano accordions.

Yet, once again, enthusiasts are at work to restore and revive. One London maker still produces a dozen concertinas a year, and restores many more old ones, now antiques. Players have founded a concertina newsletter to help keep the instrument's music alive. And the pop world too has taken notice and made use of concertinas in the backing of folk records.

Players claim that it improves the tone to swing the instrument as they play, and they often find it irresistible to tap their feet too.

Concertina

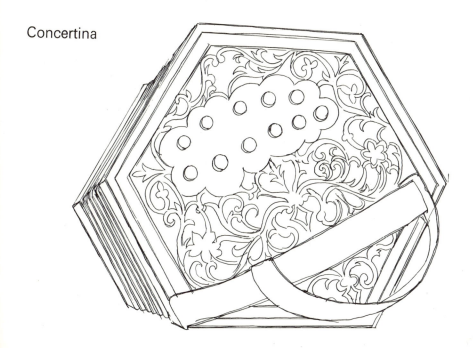

Piano Accordion

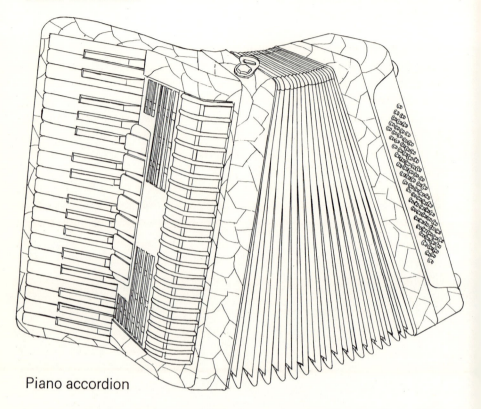

Piano accordion

The accordion became popular early in this century, using steel reeds which sounded at a steady pitch. The most popular version today is played by a small keyboard, like a piano's. The "squeeze box" is held in two hands, and often accompanies dancing. The player's right hand uses the keyboard. The left hand works the bellows and also some buttons, which can sound chords.

BRASS INSTRUMENTS

Brass is a technical term used for all the wind instruments which used to be made of brass, although other metals are used now. There are two main families. Instruments in the horn family, originally based on an animal horn, have a horn-style funnel mouthpiece and a conical bore, and give a mellow bland tone. By contrast, instruments in the trumpet family have a more strident voice, a cup type mouthpiece and a cylindrical bore, and were first made from hollow bones or canes.

A good way to observe all the instruments being played is to watch a Salvation Army band, a school band or a military band, which may have other instruments too. Notes are produced by vibrating the lips as the player blows. This vibration is passed into the column of air within the instrument. It vibrates and sounds, just as a violin string and a woodwind reed do. There should not be great pressure; the air should go straight into the instrument. The way the lips are applied to the mouthpiece is called the embouchure.

Originally, on an old "natural" trumpet, the trumpeter could only play in the key which corresponded to its length; this is called its fundamental. But any note sounded is accompanied by other

Playing brass instruments

 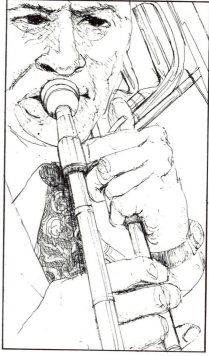

overtones, or harmonics. This is easier for you to hear within the echoing chime of a bell. A brass player alters the tension of his lips to sound his instrument's harmonics. However, the instruments you will see today have been given various mechanisms, crooks, slides and valves, to change their pitch more easily.

Tongueing is an important part of the technique of brass playing. In normal playing, the tongue moves as when you say "t". For quick passages, the tongue moves as for "tk" and "tkt", and this is double or triple tongueing. To play smooth *legato* notes, the player's lips and tongue are in a position like whistling. For low notes the tongue will be flat in the mouth, as when you say "ah"; and it will arch up as for "ee" when higher notes are sounded. Clearly, breath control is absolutely essential for a brass player.

Hunting horn

French horn

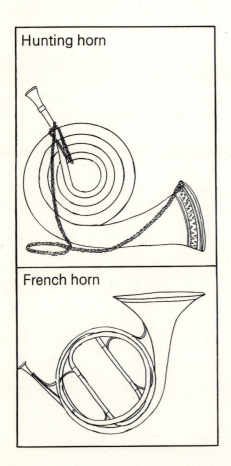

Modern horn

Horn

Early in the eighteenth century, natural horns were given crooks, additional lengths of tube, fitted into a socket which replaced the mouthpiece. Then they could play in more than one key. During that century, Anton Hampel experimented by putting his hand into the bell. First he found it acted as a mute, limiting vibration, then he also noted that he could change the note's pitch as well.

Valve horns, the kind used in today's orchestras, were made from about 1815, and with these the players could play every note in the scale. The valves changed the sounding length of tube without the frequent changes of crook which had formerly been necessary. There are tenor and baritone horns, and flugel horns, which are valve bugles.

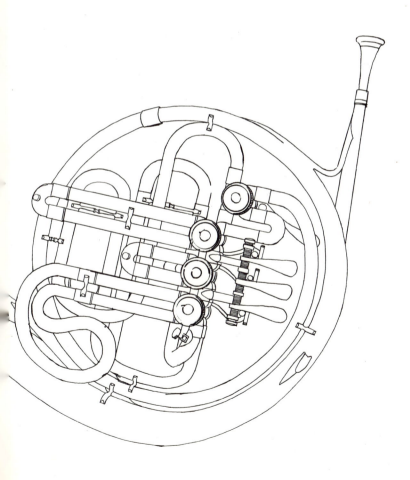

Bugle

This treble instrument's sound will be known to you from its time-honoured use in signalling; for instance, playing "Wakey Wakey" or sounding the Last Post at a funeral. These calls also demonstrate to you a "natural" wind instrument's limited range of notes.

Early bugles were horn-shaped. After 1800, they adopted the folded trumpet shape. A keyed bugle was invented, replacing the earlier wind instrument called a serpent. This bugle, the ophicleide, was in turn mostly replaced by the tuba.

Cavalry
bugle

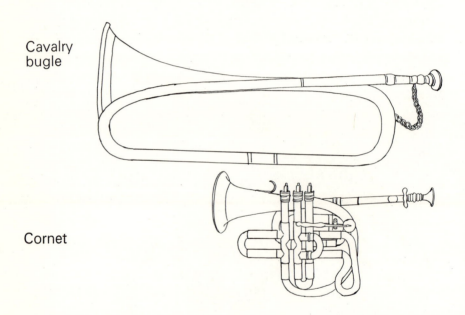

Cornet

Cornet

This instrument is based on a French circular post horn. Three valves were added, and it was very popular in the nineteenth century.

Today there is also the cornett, a revived old instrument originally made of wood or ivory bound with leather, but played like a brass instrument, with a cup-shaped mouthpiece. The six finger and one thumb holes are reminiscent of woodwind instruments. Its sound blends well with voices, as in the music of the early operas of Monteverdi (1567–1643).

Tuba

A tuba player may also use the splendid name of bombardist. A tuba is basically a deep-toned brass instrument, with valves and a cupped mouthpiece. The tenor instrument is also known as a euphonium, and the bass as a bombardon.

The American "March King", John Philip Sousa (1854–1932), invented the Sousaphone, a tuba curled round the player for marching. He believed that a good march should inspire a man with a wooden leg to step out.

Enthusiastic brass players have searched in old scores for new works to play from the fifteenth, sixteenth and seventeenth centuries, and with this enlarged repertory have been able to build up concerts full of variety, forming brass ensembles such as the one led by Philip Jones.

Playing the euphonium

Trumpets

The modern valve trumpet was developed after many experiments and could play with ease real melodies. Wagner used twelve in *Tannhäuser*.

The right hand controls three pistons which can alter the sounding pitch three times, by opening up extra loops of air to the main trumpet's air column.

A pear-shaped "mute" can be put into the trumpet's bell to soften its tone. Some jazz players use their hats. For superb playing, listen to the legendary Louis Armstrong (Satchmo) in a song such as "Hello Dolly". His trumpet sings as freely as a bird.

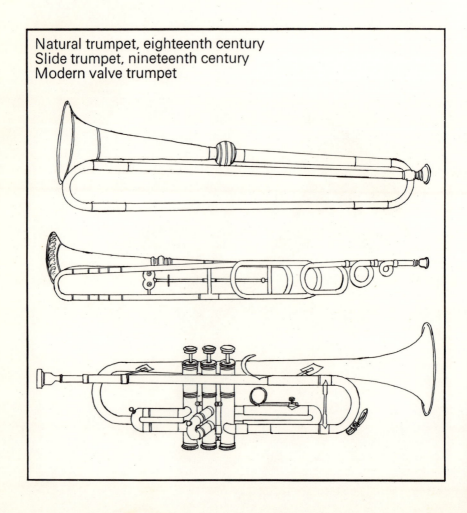

Natural trumpet, eighteenth century
Slide trumpet, nineteenth century
Modern valve trumpet

Trombone

This also is a popular instrument in jazz, and you can see the player "choosing" his pitch carefully by his use of the slide, which moves through seven positions. Each extension sounds harmonics a semitone lower. The cupped mouthpiece is larger than a trumpet's, and the player's lips themselves act as a vibrating reed.

There are various sizes of trombone: soprano, alto, tenor, the most popular, bass and double-bass.

To hear the varied use of brass instruments you can dip into the music of *The Ring*, an opera cycle by Wagner (1813–83). Also Brahms (1833–97) wrote a beautiful trio for horn, violin and piano, which shows the capabilities of the instrument.

Trombone player

7 Mechanical Instruments

MUSIC PRODUCED BY mechanical means has its own fascination. It almost seems magical that by setting a mechanism to work music is released from boxes, as if it had been hiding secretly. For his private delight, a man who can play no instrument, read no note of music, can summon an invisible genie to perform faultlessly. As early as the sixteenth century, Leonardo da Vinci made a mechanical spinet and drums. Craftsmen brought painstaking ingenuity to creating traditional instruments played mechanically, and also extraordinary musical clocks, contrivances and puppets.

Carillons

The earliest carillons or chimes were made to tell the time. Hour glasses and sun dials were not transportable. Workers in the fields would hear bells from churches, and the wealthy and privileged were able to employ musicians to mark the passing of the day. These men would play fanfares at regular intervals, sounding out from high towers. Music was used in this way as early as the fourteenth century.

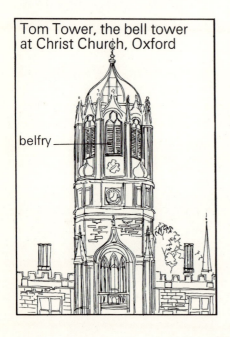

Tom Tower, the bell tower at Christ Church, Oxford

belfry

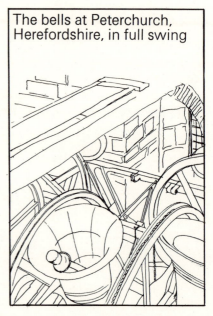

The bells at Peterchurch, Herefordshire, in full swing

74

When the simplest form of weight-driven clock mechanism was introduced, this clockwork was adopted, replacing men. The music was made by a set of bells of varying sizes which chimed different notes. Many such early bell towers still survive, and you can hear the carillons floating their tunes and striking the hours over the level land of Holland.

This labour-saving device soon suggested artistic possibilities to inventors. They aimed to produce music for pleasure, without using skilled musicians at all. Clockwork mechanisms were refined, and reduced to a smaller scale. They were then manageable for a new, indoor use.

Organ Clocks

Miniature versions of outdoor clock towers were made, and some of the earlier ones combined the traditional sets of small bells with organ pipes. Handel wrote a set of pieces for an organ clock which had bells and pipes.

Some clocks were also given moving figures or dancing dolls, fixed on cog wheels so that they were geared to dance in time to the music.

Haydn, Mozart, Beethoven and Schubert all wrote music for the organ clock. Some were called flute clocks, because of their flute-like tone. Often they were found in inns, and played to entertain guests.

The music of these clocks has especial value for us today: it is an equivalent of our gramophone records. For they play the music to us exactly as it was performed during the lifetime of the composers. Certain "twiddles" of notes, or ornaments, were not then written out in their entirety, but are preserved in the living sounds from the clockmaker's intricate work.

Barrel Organ

This was often a street instrument, played by Italian organ grinders with pet monkeys perched on their shoulders. Or it was found accompanying the singing in small churches which had no organ. In the first half of the nineteenth century, a church barrel organ might have four interchangeable wooden barrels, about nine inches in diameter, playing ten hymns each and the national anthem.

Organ grinder

Before the days of turning a barrel organ's handle, a man might have led the singing by sounding the required first note with a "pitch pipe". This was a wooden pipe, about eighteen inches long, with a whistle mouthpiece and a slider at the other end, to select the right pitch.

Today you would be most likely to see a barrel organ in a museum. But large barrel organs on wheels, sometimes pulled along by a bicycle from place to place, are still used for collecting money from passers-by in the streets of Amsterdam.

Fairground organs with their "rides" were once lit and powered by steam-generated electricity. Enthusiasts have restored them and you can see and hear them at steam fairs, even today, when most fairs only have loudspeaker music.

A barrel organ works in this way. The steady turning of a cranked handle pumps a bellows, which rotates the barrel within. From this barrel there are projections which act on keys, which open valves and these in turn control pipes. At the same time, the bellows will be blowing air through the pipes to make them sound. The projecting pins are like U-shaped staples, of differing lengths. They determine the duration of each note sounded.

For example, the largest staple would open a valve for the length of a long semibreve or whole note; the smallest would last

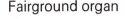

Fairground organ

only for one short semiquaver or sixteenth note. The barrel organ "chooses" pitch by means of a series of keys, one for each note it can play.

Street Piano

The street piano is the nineteenth-century version of the mechanical spinet. It is a simple upright piano, whose keyboard has been replaced by a long barrel, which the handle at the side rotates. The strings are stretched vertically. Pins on the barrel make the hammers strike the strings, just as if someone were pressing the keys down with his fingers.

Sustaining notes was a problem, so instead of holding down a key,

Street piano

as a player would, the street piano makers resorted to a quick repetition of a single note. This produced a strident jangling noise, which is characteristic of the instrument, and makes it successful for open-air playing in the street.

A Professor Babbage, who invented the calculating machine, did not enjoy the omnipresent popularity of these instruments, and in 1861 recorded and complained that his work was interrupted by six brass bands and ninety-six street pianos and organs in only ninety days.

A second handle shifted the barrel, and changed the tune, which might be one of ten, including such popular numbers as "Santa Lucia", "Sunshine Waltz", and "Sing a Song of Sixpence".

Organs with Reeds

Sometimes, instead of organ pipes, the sound was produced from single vibrating reeds, through which wind was forced, rather like a mouth organ.

The serinette or bird-organ was a miniature organ, only about six inches square, worked by turning a handle. Its short high-pitched tune was used to teach captive birds to sing.

In the mechanical spinet, the instrument maker reproduced the effects of a player's fingers by projections on a rotating cylinder.

Player Pianos

There were attempts late in the eighteenth century to make "self-acting" pianos, using barrels. Then, following experiments with organs and harmoniums, perforated sheets of cardboard or rolls of paper were used to control the works of the piano and produce tunes. The pianola was patented in 1897, by an American.

The pianola's paper roll is made to rotate by foot pedals. It passes over a tracker-bar which has corresponding holes; they are connected by a number of tubes with the normal hammer mechanism of the piano. Loud and soft playing are controlled by the foot-operated blowing, and hand levers as well.

Early in this century, the "Reproducing Piano" became enormously popular, and was made by many manufacturers. These instruments can reproduce the exact performances of a player on their rolls. A pianist would play, and holes would be punched mechanically in a master roll, later copied. Naturally, the rolls are now collector's pieces, because from them we can hear exactly how such legendary pianists as Rachmaninof interpreted music before the days of accurate recording by the gramophone. You can actually hear the playing re-recorded on discs.

Not only are there arrangements of orchestral music as well as piano music on rolls, but some composers, such as Stravinsky (1882–1971), have written directly for the player piano, no longer tied to what eight fingers and two thumbs can do with the instrument.

An early player piano

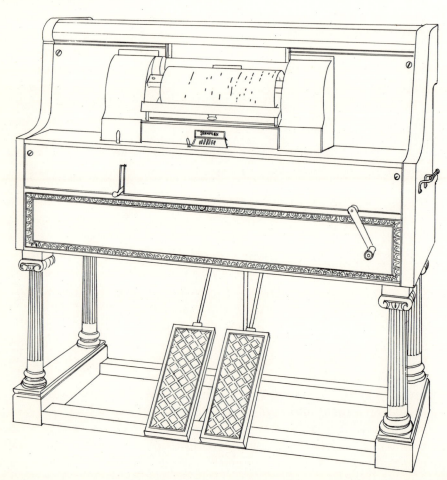

MUSICAL BOXES

The musical box is, strictly speaking, an instrument in its own right, and *not* merely a mechanized version of an ordinary musical instrument. The instrument is a steel or metal comb, whose teeth are graded in length, and, when vibrated, sound a scale of notes. The comb's teeth or tongues are plucked upwards by protruding pins on a rotating cylinder or disc. The position of these pins determines the tune which is played. The brass teeth have a piece of lead on their underside to control the rate of vibration. The treble teeth vibrate so quickly they do not need resonators. To stop a tooth vibrating, a damper made of a short length of thin flat steel wire is pinned under its end. If it is not dampened, it will chatter or grunt. The clockwork movement is set working by a winding handle or switch.

The first version was probably invented by a Swiss, Antoine Favre, round about 1796. Later developments brought a horizontal comb, the teeth at first screwed separately, then later all together. Some boxes had two or even more combs. At first, Favre's invention was only applied to snuffboxes, watches and seals by the

Early musical box interior, about 1810

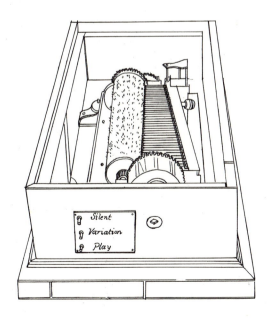

Mechanical bird in snuffbox

Musical watch interior showing
the movement, about 1880

Pistol with mechanical bird

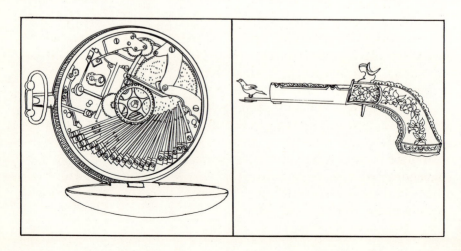

group of watchmakers who congregated at Geneva in the early years of the nineteenth century.

The mechanism of boxes is intricate, and pins can be bent and broken if a "run" occurs when part of the mechanical movement breaks, and the cylinder revolves suddenly until the spring which controls it is unwound. Damaged cylinders have to be repinned by hand.

Later musical boxes were made quite separately in all sizes and designs and with elaborate decorations. By about 1870 they had reached their peak. On shifting the position of the barrel different tunes could be played. Some boxes had interchangeable barrels, though these had to be rather large and expensive; some had bells and drums.

One of the most ingenious creations was the singing bird snuffbox.

A button is moved at the front of the box, and the oval lid lifts up to show a tiny bird, about an inch long. The mechanism "sings" for the bird as it flaps its wings and moves head and tail before the song ends, and the bird falls back into its box.

Naturally by now such delicate works of art are collectors' pieces. And so are *Automata*. These are objects which move by clockwork, and sometimes are accompanied by music. A rabbit appears to music from an unfolding lettuce. Lions leap and roar. A puppet pianist and fiddler play while a monkey dances between them. Beautifully dressed dolls perform to each other. And birds cheep and flutter within gilt cages.

There was great variety. Late in the nineteenth century, musical boxes worked by revolving steel discs, or music sheets, instead of cylinders playing the combs were developed. These were Symphonions, Polyphons and Reginas. Mechanical achievements were exploited, and finally the phonograph was invented.

In their heyday, musical boxes were treasures of craftsmanship, and also a means of bringing the popular music of the nineteenth century into people's own drawing rooms. Their music was completely clockwork accurate, maddeningly or magically so, depending on your viewpoint.

Musical movements are still made today, as toys or in clocks, mainly in Switzerland and Japan.

8 Electronic Instruments

IF THEY ARE working well, machines give flawless performances. Musical mechanisms are not variable, like human players. They do not have "off days". For the composer, this can be a challenge. No human interpreter comes between his idea of his music and its playing, when the instrument works by clockwork or electric power.

The composer is his own interpreter in electronic music. He creates a composition in sounds. Basically, two electric currents, whose vibrating frequency differs, are combined together. This interference, one with the other, produces beats, which are too rapid to make a true sound until they are passed through some sort of loud-speaker. Then the sound engineer can make pure sounds, rather like a tuning fork noise, or "square waves", which can be all sorts of buzzings, hissings and bubblings. These he can mix together by using several tape-recorders and playing the sounds at different speeds, or even backwards. You will know the difference speed can make to sounds if you have, by mistake, started to play a record meant to be played at thirty-three and a third revolutions a minute at forty-five instead.

These somewhat weird tones and sounds were at first used to give atmosphere, for instance in supernatural or science fiction stories on radio or television. The B.B.C. officially set up a Radiophonic Workshop in 1958 to produce special effects and conduct experiments.

Today, schools, universities and some private owners have their own sound studios, full of complex machines: oscillators or generators, reverberation machines, tape recorders, filters, mixers, Moog synthesizers and many more gadgets to manipulate sounds. Tristram Carey and Daphne Oram both compose electronic music and have their own studios, and you may hear their work broadcast.

Musique Concrète

This French name translates slightly comically into English as "concrete music". The name was given by French experimenters to the manipulation of ordinary sounds. Usually, sounds from objects such as bottles or jugs, as well as conventional instruments, are recorded. Then these sounds are juggled with, on tapes. But there have been and still are many experiments with varying patterns of sound. Many different names are given, but in a sense they all produce a sort of synthetic music.

Semi-Electric Instruments

Again, there have been many experiments to aid or modify the sound of traditional instruments by electric power. For instance, there are pipeless electric organs such as the Hammond organs, producing tone from rotating discs with pick-ups.

The electric instrument you will know best is the electric guitar. Instead of vibrating from a soundboard, the sound is picked up electronically and passed to an amplifier and then out of a loud-speaker, rather like a radio.

Combining the traditional sounds of Indian tablas with music from an electronic workshop

9 The Reproduction of Music

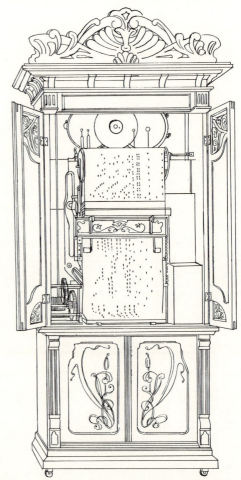

Piano orchestrion
with percussion

Below: HMV dog
Disc
Symphonion

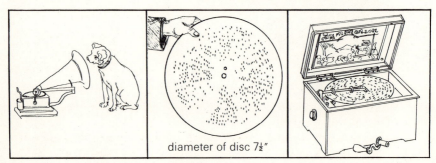

diameter of disc 7½"

MECHANICAL INSTRUMENTS HAD sought to imprison musical perfection in boxes and clocks as early as the sixteenth century. By the nineteenth century, the piano roll was able to capture individual performances. Such pianists as Paderewski and Rachmaninof cut rolls for leading companies making player pianos, at the height of their popularity between 1915 and 1925. It must be admitted, however, that the performance we can hear from rolls cannot quite produce as the gramophone did nuances of touch and the pulse of the music.

Today the gramophone can reproduce any sound of speech or music and record it permanently to be repeated at any time required on equipment which has become a commonplace possession for millions of people. They can even compare different interpretations of one piece. This has been an amazing progression, with far-reaching effects on the practice and enjoyment of music all over the world.

Yet the success of the gramophone industry helped to blight the musical box industry. By the end of the First World War in 1918, the voice of the old musical box was almost drowned by that of the player piano, the nickelodeon and the dance organ. The twentieth century succumbed to the latest novelty charm of gramophone and wireless, epitomized by the famous listening dog trade mark on H.M.V., "His Master's Voice".

Clockwork music, formerly heard in so many homes and cafés, was no longer part of everyday life.

The makers of musical boxes did not give way without struggling, and many large firms produced dual machines, like the short-lived Gramo-Polyphon, a gramophone and polyphon in one. Others turned over to produce gramophones, or left the business.

SOME FORBEARS OF THE GRAMOPHONE

When a new type of musical box was invented round about 1886, playing easily interchangeable discs instead of cylinders, it launched a boom of popularity. Made under the name of Symphonion from 1890, it was sold in versions from toys at five shillings (25p), up to fifty guinea models, with the discs or metallic tune plates costing up to two shillings (10p).

Also there were Reginas, Armorettes, and Polyphons fitted with visible machinery, two thousand tunes to choose from and a penny-in-the-slot mechanism to make them pay their way in bars and restaurants.

To set at work yourself, there were the player piano, the Orchestrion self player organ, and the Aeolian Orchestrelle reed organ, by the use of stops imitating all the orchestra's instruments in its performance, and sometimes costing hundreds of pounds or dollars. These could be played by keyboard or by perforated paper rolls.

More sturdy, and very popular, were the American Roller Organs, played by pinned wooden rollers, which acted on valve keys, and were driven by gearing which also worked the bellows.

But all these elaborate self-playing mechanical wonders—and there were hundreds competing for attention in the market—were to fade into obscurity.

Left: Polyphon
Below: American roller organ, 1896

THE HISTORY OF THE GRAMOPHONE

Sound Recording: The Clockwork Voice

Ideas had been put forward by E. L. Scott (the Phonautograph) and Charles Cros (the Paléophone) and others earlier, but it was the making of a model talking machine, the Phonograph, in 1877 which launched in a practical way the sort of instrument we now call a record player.

Thomas Edison had been working in America to improve the telegraph transmitter. He worked out that the vibrations caused by sound on the diaphragm of a telephone might be "recorded" by an attached stylus as it vibrated, indenting or marking a steadily moving strip of paraffined paper. This arose because Edison was slightly deaf, and attached a needle to the receiver's diaphragm to help him check the loudness of sounds.

The marked paper led him to try instead a rotating grooved cylinder wrapped round with a piece of tin foil, which the recording needle marked with a pattern of sound vibrations. There were two diaphragm and needle units, one for recording, the other for playing back. The speaker shouted into the mouthpiece. He adjusted the reproducer, turned the cylinder again with its handle, and heard his own voice recognizably. Edison, the story goes, pronounced, "Mary had a little lamb", and, on hearing it played back said, "I was never so taken aback in my life."

Tinfoil phonograph, 1877

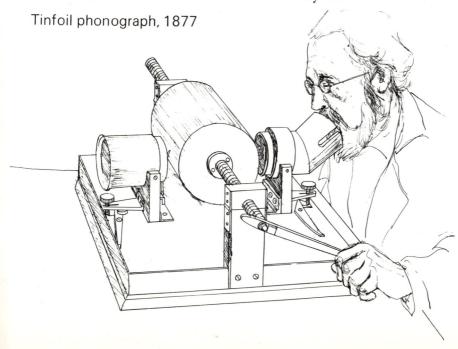

Admired as a scientific instrument in England, it was given a weighted flywheel to make rotation more even, a clockwork motor to drive the cylinder, then in about 1883 a spring motor.

The development of the talking machine was complicated by many technical difficulties and rivalries between inventors and this brief account has to be selective.

During 1878, Edison displayed various models of phonographs to the public, trying out, for instance, flat discs, and listing the business and private uses his invention could have. But in fact the tin foil wore out after about six playings. The reproduction was metallic, lasted a little more than a minute and was only just distinguishable. The curious crowds drifted away from a seven day wonder, and Edison became immersed in developing the electric lamp.

Other inventors, however, took up the concept. Alexander Graham Bell, who invented the telephone, produced by 1885 the Graphophone. In this instrument, the sound impressions were cut on the wax-coated surface of a cardboard cylinder, following many experiments with cylinders, discs and tapes.

Then Emile Berliner produced in America the gramophone, a rival to the phonograph and Graphophone, which was developed from experiments with a Phonautograph, and a reproducing machine.

First manufactured in Germany as a toy (in 1889) the Berliner hand-driven or electric gramophone, with hearing tubes if required,

Left: Berliner reproducing machine, 1888
Below: Berliner hand-driven gramophone, 1893

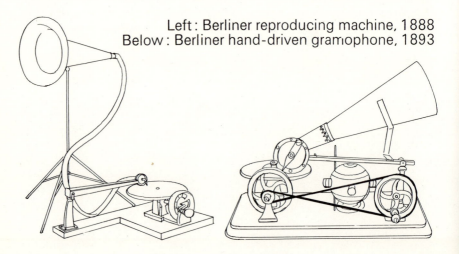

was marketed in America in 1893. Berliner had replaced cylinders with seven-inch discs pressed in hard rubber, later changed to a shellac mixture.

There followed a spate of experiments and inventions, accompanied by ruthless competition. The talking machine dealer often sold bicycles as well in his shop. There were numerous models to choose from, many exported from Germany. Records were tried in various sizes. Some played on one side only; some worked from the inside towards the outer edge of the disc.

The horn was embellished or hidden. Disc machines began to look like ordinary furniture.

In the electric gramophone, the needle communicated the sound vibration from voice or instrument to a "pick-up", whose electromagnet sent electric vibrations to be amplified by valves. These vibrations were passed to a loudspeaker.

In very early recording sessions, each record was a "master", made direct, and a singer might reproduce twelve records, singing into twelve horns, then repeat that as often as he could endure. There is a special quality you can observe in early recorded orchestral playing, because a small band would be squashed together to get near to the horn, almost sitting on each others' knees as they played. The sound is uneven and scratchy, yet somehow exciting, and it is easy to imagine the thrill of paying a nickel in an American store and hearing the wonderful phonograph perform through your ear tubes.

The Angelus, 1906   Puck model for both cylinders and discs, 1905

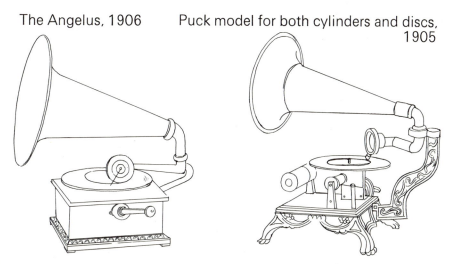

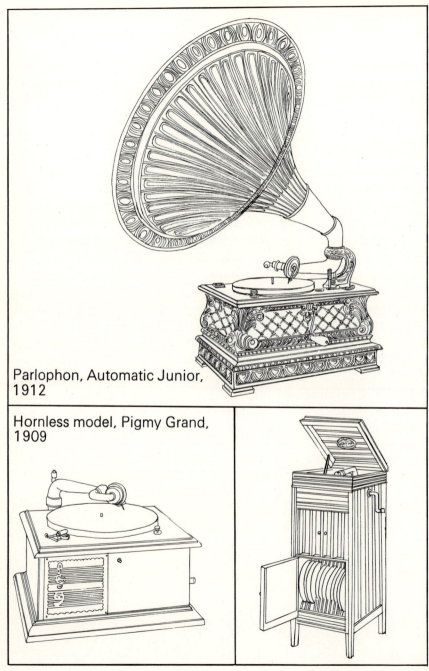

Parlophon, Automatic Junior,
1912

Hornless model, Pigmy Grand,
1909

Mignonette, 1912

The great singer Caruso first consented to record his voice in 1902. He made one hundred and fifty-four records up to 1921. He earned a fortune for himself, and established the record as a serious means of propagating musical performances.

Records were made double-sided from 1905. Also in that year there was a delectable toy talking machine made, with edible chocolate discs.

Selections of music were announced. Sometimes jokes and advertisements were included in the performance. Nellie Melba recorded from 1904, and her twelve-inch discs were one guinea each. When the famous opera singer Patti agreed to sing, she insisted that the recorders should attend at her Welsh castle and wait until she felt ready to sing. The gramophone company then advertised her pink labelled records with streamers flying from their shops, announcing: "Patti is Singing Here Today".

Debussy thought that the gramophone was able to give music complete immortality, and in 1904 agreed to accompany some of his songs in a Paris studio.

The gramophone prospered, and extended its range from solo performers to attempts at orchestral works and even complete operas. The Marathon disc made between 1912 and 1915, and played for sixteen and a half minutes, was an early attempt to produce a long-playing record. Serious listeners founded their own

Children listening
to a phonograph
in the 1890's

magazine, *The Gramophone*, in 1923, to discuss recordings and recording instruments. (It is still thriving today.)

Electrical recording had its first commercial successes in 1925, with a massed choir record and a foxtrot, "Let it Rain, Let it Pour", for dancing. The range was extended. In 1936, Toscanini made a set of recordings conducting the New York Philharmonic-Symphony. The musical quality was so exceptional that they have recently been reissued.

In the thirties also, the juke box was responsible for popularizing hundreds and selling thousands of popular swing records, such as Benny Goodman's "One O'Clock Jump", at the drop of a coin.

Yet before this there had been another invention to excite music lovers, the radio. By 1922, manufacturers had already begun to produce combination phonograph-radios which sold well.

Stollwerck toy talking machine
playing a chocolate disc, 1905

THE RADIO

As early as 1830, Michael Faraday discovered that electric energy could be passed through the ether/air from one electrical circuit to another. Further experiments led to the discovery that signals without wires, or waves, could be transmitted and received. The

Dame Nellie Melba
broadcasting in 1920

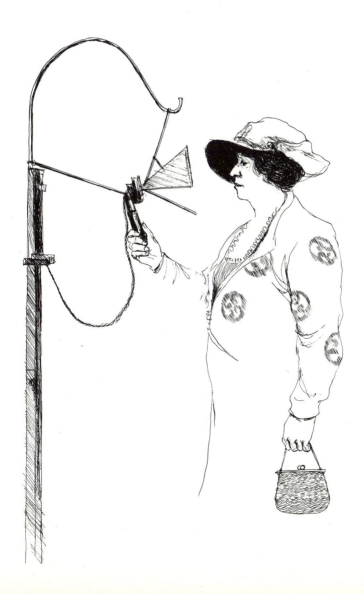

British Post Office in 1895 gave the Italian Marconi opportunities to work on a wireless telegraphic system. By 1898 twelve miles were bridged. In 1901, Marconi sent out messages 1,800 miles. Countless experiments were being made in many countries. Wireless telephony was used between ships in the First World War. In 1919, American amateurs began broadcasting to each other. In 1920, an experimental English broadcasting station was opened; in 1922 the British Broadcasting Company was formed, and later (1927) renamed the British Broadcasting Corporation.

The radio brought into people's homes vastly increased listening opportunities in music. Once they owned a set (and, in some countries, paid a licence), listeners had access to a whole new world of sound which today we take for granted, with tiny transistors tucked into our pockets. Music was even more readily available than with the gramophone, which needed much more than the turn of a switch.

Early radios were run on electricity from the mains. Now battery radios with transistors (smaller and not likely to become hot as valves do), which enable the size of the receiver to be much reduced, are mass-produced, and relatively cheap.

RECORD PLAYERS

The gramophone too has been modernized and today's record player strives to reproduce music with sound of "high fidelity", shortened as "hifi". There are many varieties of equipment

Diagram of a record player

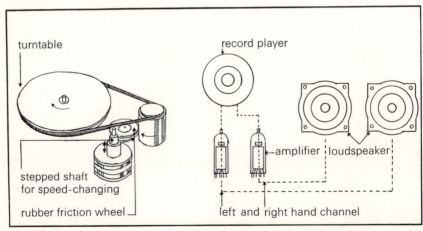

turntable

record player

stepped shaft
for speed-changing

amplifier   loudspeaker

rubber friction wheel

left and right hand channel

rivalling each other. Stereo records are made by two separate microphones. The pickup is designed to produce two signals. Quadraphonics produces music as if it were from the four corners of the room, using say fifty microphones on thirty-two track tape, and separating out the sound before the listener hears it, just as if he had two pairs of ears!

Doubtless there will be other expensive refinements on the basic equipment: a turntable with a drive mechanism, a pickup mounted on a tone arm, an amplifier and loudspeaker, sending out sound. These parts are sometimes separated, as they can affect each other by such things as vibrations, and spoil the tone.

The record player is producing sound waves from the disc's grooves. These grooves have been cut in wavy patterns on the plastic "unbreakable" disc by a cutter transmitting sound vibrations from the air. The disc is rotated at the same speed as the recording, and reproduces the original sound vibrations, to be amplified. Older standard records rotated at 78 revolutions per minute. Long playing records rotate at $33\frac{1}{3}$ r.p.m. or at 45 r.p.m. for extended play.

But the disc system, with all its excellence, has a strong rival, the tape-recorder.

MAGNETIC RECORDING ON TAPE

Pressure waves in the air created by musical sound make a variety of vibrations, which are picked up by a microphone and amplified.

Diagram of a tape recorder

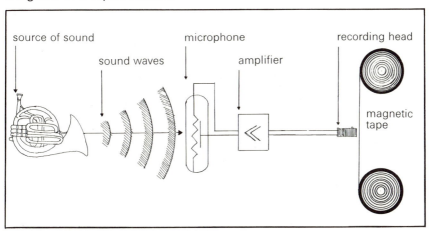

source of sound   microphone   recording head

sound waves   amplifier

magnetic tape

These electric signals are able to produce variations in the strength of a magnetic field, in this case a tape. Today's tapes are often made of plastic, coated with powdered red iron oxide. An electromagnet in the recording head marks the tape with magnetic variations. The electric current passing through the recording head magnetizes the particles in the tape. To reproduce the sound, the tape is passed over a similar reproducing head at the recording speed.

This device is useful for home or amateur use, when musicians can make their own recordings, then, if they wish, erase the music from the tape, and use it again. Tapes are sold in cassettes, and now compete with records, which it is possible they may one day replace.

TELEVISION

Television was invented during the thirties, but its large-scale development was held up during the Second World War (1939–1945). Although the reproduction of sound is not yet comparable with the high standard of recorded discs and tapes, visual music, teaching and performance, is well demonstrated alongside sound, again within people's homes instead of on a special occasion in lecture or concert hall.

MUSICAL RECORDERS MAKING NEW MUSIC

As well as the straightforward use of tapes for recording sound, there have been experiments with tape-recorders played at different speeds and backwards, producing strange new sounds. Composers have not hesitated to make use of these in compositions, and to combine them with the sounds of traditional instruments.

Some people deplore the omnipresence of music today. They complain that it is so easily available, on record player, radio or television, that there is a danger of no longer *listening* at all. The music can become inaudible background, like an unseen wallpaper. But this seems an ungrateful reaction to the incredibly swift development of many painstaking inventions into sources of musical familiarity and delight, bringing the best music the world has to offer to be savoured at leisure in our homes.

10 The Written Language of Music

IT IS NOT easy to capture sounds and put them down on paper. The earliest musicians did not attempt to do so. Long before any written records, early music was taught by ear, by one generation copying another, the taught adding little quirks, variations and alterations to make the handed-down music their own.

The development of the musical notation you can see printed today was a very gradual process. Before the invention of printing in about 1440, the records were handwritten manuscripts. The first attempts were signs placed above the Latin texts of church music, like shorthand reminders to someone who already was familiar with the music, telling him when the tune moved up or down.

These signs were called neumes. They were given different shapes, to make their meaning clearer, and during the ninth and tenth centuries there were many attempts to note down *pitch*, how high or low a note was to be.

Some time before the year 1000, an unknown scribe drew above the text a red line, representing the note F. Then he placed neumes on it, above or below it, so that the few notes sounding near F could be accurately conveyed by signs. Gradually this idea was developed and a yellow line was added above the red, to represent C. Then two black lines, one each side of the F line, were added, and with these four making a "stave" or staff, many traditional melodies could be written down.

The next improvement was the introduction of clefs or keys. These were the letters F and C placed on the stave to mark where those notes were to be for the particular piece. That meant more tunes could be written down. These signs were elaborated by scribes, as was the G clef, which appeared in the thirteenth century. They all survive today, though altered.

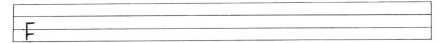

Note F is the second line from the bottom.

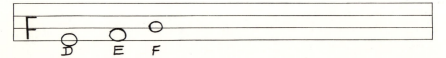

Nowadays we use, on a five line stave, the C clef. This is movable, and is used, for instance, to write viola parts as the alto clef, with middle C on the third line.

More commonly, we have fixed the G or treble clef for notes mainly above middle C, and the F or bass clef for lower notes. To write down notes off the stave short ledger lines are added. Look at a piece of printed piano music. The right hand plays what is written for the treble clef, and the left the bass clef.

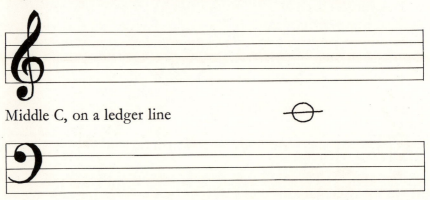

Middle C, on a ledger line

This method of calling notes by letters came originally from the Greek and Roman systems. But you can appreciate that hand-written manuscripts, from widely scattered churches and monasteries, were often very unalike in appearance, as individual scribes attempted to write down more and more clearly what was to be sung.

The next challenge, to try to note time values, how long each note was to be held, began to be met late in the twelfth century. It may have been influenced by the rhythmic beats of secular dance music, but measurable music was now recorded, quite apart from the "natural" length of words sung. By the fourteenth century, note signs had developed which are fairly like our own written notes today.

Today's Notes

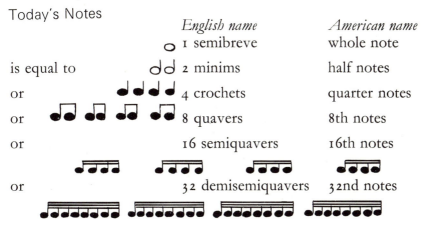

		English name	American name
		1 semibreve	whole note
is equal to		2 minims	half notes
or		4 crochets	quarter notes
or		8 quavers	8th notes
or		16 semiquavers	16th notes
or		32 demisemiquavers	32nd notes

This timed music was at first broken up by lines or bars drawn vertically across the stave to make it easier to read, during the sixteenth and seventeenth centuries. Rhythm was meant to be freer than in later music, which came to be divided up into measures or bars of *equal* length, as you can see in this nursery rhyme.

Baa baa black sheep, have you any wool?

Time signatures, denoting how many beats in the bar, added to the complications. This nursery tune is in "common" time, four crochet beats to the bar. There is a lot to convey, by written symbols; even, for example, when there is no sound, that silence must be recorded as a "rest" of a length equivalent to a note, such as ♩ , a quaver rest. A pause too needs its own sign ⌢ . There are many details (such as sharps ♯ , and flats ♭) to be learnt in the reading of music, and there have been many attempts to simplify it, without much success.

For composers are still struggling to convey to players exactly what they mean to be sounded. There are various instructions, about speed and style of performance, often by tradition in Italian, which they can give, and there is a list of common ones on page 211. Yet there remains an indescribable element which defies writing down. It is that "life" in the composition which composer-players or conductors have been able to demonstrate to their musicians: just how they want the black and white notes to be translated into ordered sound.

Of course, that is part of the fascination of music, that for each playing it has to be made again, raised up from the dead printed page.

The first bars of Beethoven's Sonata in C minor, Opus 111, in Beethoven's hand and the modern printed form

COMPOSING AND NOTING DOWN

There is something deeply satisfying in what you find out for yourself. In some schools today, children are discovering music by composing it. Of course, they do not compose great works: they experiment with sounds. (*See also* Synthesizers, p. 84). Neither their teachers nor they close their minds to what is new and different: they open their ears. For them, music is a voyage of exploration. What they discover is that they can make for themselves a sort of first music. And this leads them to enjoy equally experimental modern music, and then to learn from the great "masters" of traditional music what they found in their day.

How this is done varies considerably, but, for instance, one school had a large water tank full of fish. They set about describing it in words and music, illustrating the fishes with the sounds of bubble blowing in a metal jug, striking and wiping across a xylophone

with its sticks, plopping a cymbal into a plastic dustbin half full of water (then draining it on a plastic sheet) and chiming with chime bars.

Another group did special sound effects while a story about space was read aloud. They tapped wine bottles of differing sizes, empty or full. They blew down the spout of a watering can, or an old washing-machine tube. They scraped a metal cheese grater with a fork, a dulcimer with a knife, a bicycle wheel with a metal stick. They evolved many strange and effective noises. Most of these could *not* be written down in the ordinary musical notation. The players wanted a record of what they had made up. A tape recording could not be kept for ever. So they began to draw the sounds, for instance, zigzags for stroking across strings

"ch" for shakers, "pop pop" for recorders,

for up   for down

numbers for how many times drums (or tin trays with panlids) had to be struck.

Dealing with drums, they might begin by drawing plain circles in sizes.

Big   Medium   Small

would then mean three beats on the big drum, one on the small, and one on the medium size.

This is the simplest kind of shorthand, just to help the memory for future performances. *How* the drums were to be beaten would be worked out in practice. In a somewhat similar way, American Indians used birch bark rolls to write down signs to remind them of their drum accompanied songs.

These graphics worked with simple effects. Gradually, as the music became more ambitious, the children wanted to express more. They felt the need to learn notes, and be able to say what pitch was to be sung.

The real excitement was that the players found that they could make and record their own music long before they could read other people's music.

Another class might divide itself into small groups of two to five, and choose their own instruments from snare drums, bongos, cymbals, xylophones, glockenspiels, psalteries, triangles and chime bars. Then they were told to try out how their instruments sounded, playing what they liked. Sometimes the teacher would give help on how an instrument worked best, but what mattered most was listening to what sound you could create. Then the groups were told to make up a piece together, and set to practise it. Even with only eighteen "composers", the noise would be considerable, and good concentration essential.

Next, each group performed, and the others commented on what they heard. Very gradually, the small groups managed to work out real patterns of sound. One might give the other players whispered cues, or count them in and out of the piece. One player might lead in with a rhythm copied by a second while another is shaking the shakers to keep time steady. The pattern might be passed on with differing rhythms, and then the group might join to make a cluster of sounds, some holding on to notes, others wavering.

The comments of the other groups might be scathing: "Is that all?" to a great drum beating, or admiringly puzzled: "I like that. I don't know why."

SOME OTHER FORMS OF NOTATION

This music making is a form of *Improvisation*. Many composers today have wanted to leave scope for the players to go on creating as they play, and so have produced more free scores than in traditional musical notation. For instance, a "sound picture" has been made to describe autumn by Dr John Paynter. High voices slowly sing words translated from a Japanese haiku: "The falling leaves fall and pile up. The rain beats on the rain." They start each phrase together, but each voice sings at his own pace, then waits, holding his last note, till the others join in, while glockenspiels and plucked violins play any notes at random very fast but very quietly, and chime bars toll notes.

Such a score uses some traditional notation, and then shows random notes by irregular dots, and an agreed repeated note by regular dots.

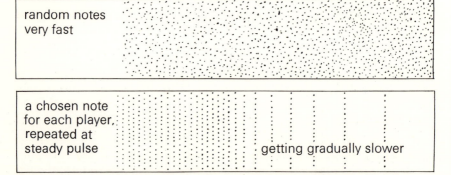

If new symbols become too complicated, needing their own glossary to explain them, then scores are troublesome, and time-consuming to read at rehearsal. One simple device, used by Penderecki (born 1933) and others, is to use an arrow for repetition of a little fragment or motif.

Some composers deliberately write only in shorthand. They write for a number of percussionists, say three to five, who choose their own instruments, which might include squeaky rubber toys and pieces of glass. Then they improvise, with or without direction from a conductor, using the score as a starting point, and deciding by ear when is the best moment to smash the pane of glass! Such composers hope, by giving their players such freedom, to have a sort of collaboration with them. The composer writes a "squiggle" just as experimenting children have done, and expects the players to fill in details of their own.

Another way of writing down music in which the structure is not fixed is to use boxes. Sections of music are printed in boxes, which can be played clockwise or anticlockwise, beginning where the player wishes. A page would look like this:

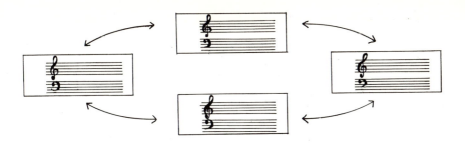

Not surprisingly, children often have a sympathy with this "made-up" music, and come to it easily.

Another form of shorthand, sometimes used today for such instruments as the guitar and mandoline, is Tablature. This system uses figures and letters to indicate chords to be played and the position of fingers on the fingerboard, instead of written notes. Look at a guitar Tutor.

Benjamin Britten has written a special sort of shorthand in his opera *Death in Venice* (1973), when the hero sings his thoughts and reads out his diary. The music written down gives only the pitch of the notes. Their length and rhythm is left to the singer, to make his singing like natural speech. (This is based on an earlier usage in the Passion music of Schütz (1585–1672).)

Other composers, such as Peter Maxwell Davies (born 1934) and Bruce Cole (born 1947), who have worked with children and written for them, have used some traditional notation. Yet they have added to it written instructions for blowing whistles, tapping the strings inside a piano, and even milk bottles with coins. They also ask for more conventional taps with brushes on drums and suspended cymbals.

There is a questing restlessness in modern music to create new sounds and then to write them down somehow, so that they can be "read" and reproduced. Even though the already rather complicated written language seems limited today, this conventional notation still has great value if you are seriously interested in music. For it can reveal to you, as you study, the musical inspiration of the acknowledged great composers of yesterday, as well as a good part of the experimental work of today.

11 Religion and Magic in Music

MUSIC DOES HAVE special qualities. It can alarm. It can soothe. It can excite both the player and the listener. This has led men to believe that music can work magic. And because music has such power to arouse emotion, it has naturally played a part in religious ceremonies, when people are striving to express their deepest feelings about man, God and the universe. This has been manifested in rites of playing, singing and dancing.

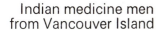

Indian medicine men
from Vancouver Island

Some instruments, such as the flute, have from ancient times been accorded magic powers. An Iron Age bone flute was excavated in Yorkshire, England, in 1951, in ancient graves. That suggested that the flute represented for the owner a personal possession not to be imitated, a sort of second voice, to be silenced at the same time as his own.

Some African tribes have believed that the music of flutes could prevent storms, make rain and encourage cows to yield milk.

Although headhunting was stopped fifty or sixty years ago in Papua, New Guinea, an Australian collector has recorded songs which hold vestiges of the tribal war dances. Up to about 1952, there were still initiation ceremonies for young warriors in the tribes' spirit houses, starting at dawn. The village elders preserved and passed down a song of ancestors, sung to music of bamboo flutes, accompanied by seed case rattles and drums. Even now, when the ceremonies are no longer observed, and young warriors are not put to the test, the ritual songs remain as folk music.

Drums have received sacrifices and been given their own food and charms. The Bible gives us a marvellous story of music's fearsome power. Gideon attacked by night a giant company of his enemies, the Midianites, with only three hundred followers. Each one, however, was "armed" with a trumpet, a torch, a water jar and a sword. Hiding the torches within the empty jars, they surrounded the camp silently. Then, when the sign was given, they blasted on their trumpets and waved lights and swords, declaiming: "The sword of the Lord and of Gideon". The effect was terrifying: their enemies panicked and retreated in confusion.

Similarly, in old India, conch shell trumpets were used to frighten enemies in battle. They are still temple instruments today.

It may be that the material of the instrument was considered especially important. Instruments made from animal bones, for instance, have been used in rituals seeking good fortune in the next hunt.

Cultivation also gathered its superstitions set to music. English wassail songs were sung as spiced ale was drunk from a wassail bowl at Christmas and New Year. On Twelfth Night, even apple trees in Somerset were wassailed by men firing their guns through the branches, pouring cider into the roots, and putting cider toast or cake in the fork while they sang to urge the tree to produce well in the coming year.

"Here's to thee, old apple tree,
Whence thou mayst bud, and whence thou mayst blow,
Whence thou mayst bear apples enow!
Hats full! Caps full! . . .
Huzza! Huzza! Huzza!"

Ancient religious ideas persist, embedded in old songs. Trinidad has given us the calypso song, the Limbo and Bongo dances, and such songs as "Ogoun Belele". The strange words reflect a belief in the god Ogoun Belele, who is everywhere, in trees, air, water and in us. The names of other deities are also called upon repeatedly, to speak for the pleading singer. The insistent drum beats accompanying the song as it calls on God bear witness to its original connection with Obi, a form of witchcraft.

In Europe, witches, feared and persecuted as anti-Christian wreakers of evil, also used music. Their sabbat was a midnight meeting of witches and sorcerers, supposed to be presided over by the devil himself. The rite would be connected with old worship of fertility, a torchlit dance of "animals", sometimes clothed, sometimes naked and masked, sometimes in deliberate mockery of church services. There was dancing and often drunkenness, so that people coming on the scene from outside were astonished at the Black Mass, danced to wild versions of local dances, with tambourine, drums, violins or bagpipes, clapping and singing. Witchcraft is still secretly practised today.

Spells and incantations are thought to have more power when chanted, and accompanied by ominous drum beats. Witch doctors use potions and music in their work to release people who believe themselves to be bewitched. The witch doctor in a Zande meeting, for instance, will divine the answers to questions when he is in a trance brought upon him by taking potions, then dancing till exhausted. While others drum and sing, he wears wooden bells at his waist and rattling seeds on his arms and legs.

There are many kinds of witch doctor, and sometimes they are women. Recordings have been made in Kenya, demonstrating a medicine man singing repeatedly to a drumming accompaniment a reassurance: "Never you mind." His power to cure is respected. He may drum to shake an evil power out of the body, or soothe a feverish child with the music of a stringed instrument. He may strike a goatskin-covered pot with a stick, play a cow horn or sing.

American Indians used songs to suggest and promote healing by influencing the patient's mind and spirit. Often songs came to the medical men in dreams, and certainly they were considered to be inspired, rather than made up. This belief is echoed by a modern Hindu musician, Gopal Sharman, who connects making music with understanding the universe and all creatures. For him, "song is an act of rising above both life and death".

In the western world, we have relearned the healing use of music for sick minds and bodies. Doctors today treat mentally ill and handicapped patients with music therapy. They bring music for listening or joining in to patients who find it pleasing and stimulating. They are almost enchanted.

We still relish music's power to excite. In the world of sport, music is used to rally the crowd to an excited mood of expectation. They may watch a performance of drum majorettes in the giant arena at baseball, or bellow songs in musical togetherness at football matches. Pop festivals entice thousands to worship new sounds.

The power of music is actually feared by some rulers who hold their power by force. If patriotic songs so move their listeners that they may be willing to fight to regain freedom, to risk their lives, then the ruthless dictator will banish the composer. He will forbid the public performance of works which express and rouse the spirit of an imprisoned people. They may appear to be simple popular songs, yet they enshrine a quintessence of national feeling.

In recent years the Greek composer, Mikis Theodorakis, was imprisoned by the Greek Colonels. His works were neither officially published nor played during their rule. Only when their harsh régime was overthrown were fifty thousand Greeks able to hear Theodorakis publicly conducting his own work for the first time in eight years. His music had become the song of freedom.

Even today, in a world dominated by the advances of scientific discovery, there remain mysterious forces, unexplained feelings, which can be expressed partially in the "magic" of music. Whether it is used to inspire awe, even terror, to heal, to enchant or to persuade, there is no doubt that music's primeval power is still alive.

12 Music to Go with Work

WHY IS MUSIC used to accompany work? Sometimes it is used to cheer the worker's spirits, to make repetition more palatable as he sings while his hands are busy.

Music with a strong rhythm may help such actions as marching. If they have no band, soldiers will whistle or sing to keep in time, and help themselves along on a route march.

To young children their games are their "work", and many are accompanied by singing, skipping or dancing. A mother's work of soothing or rocking a baby often includes the humming or singing of a lullaby. And dairy maids used to sing encouragingly to cows they milked by hand and knew by name.

The point of a work song has often been participation. It needed to be heard so that the workers could join in. It has had a long life. In ancient Greece, there were songs for drawing water and treading grapes for wine. New Zealand Maoris sang as they hauled their canoes. In the Hebrides there were songs for pulling wool to make tweed. A railroad section leader called out pulls and pushes while his men lined the track.

Many work songs are to be found as folk songs, where ordinary people unconsciously recorded their oldest stories and customs, their work and play and feelings about them. There must be at least traces of such songs in all folk lore, and it is only possible to choose some of what the great American collector Alan Lomax called "homemade hand-me-downs in words and music". There is such variety.

When American lumberjacks were tackling whole forests of trees, they sang heroic songs to give themselves strength. Similarly, in Trinidad there were songs for hauling timber and picking bananas.

> "Mary gone a – mountain
> Get yellow plantain . . .
> Highland Dey. Highland Dey."

A miner for coal cheered his hard life by singing a forty versed ballad "Down down down" as he rode in the mule car along the dark gangways, orchestrated by underground blastings and rats' scrapings. Gold miners sang of hoping to "strike it rich" and settle down.

American cowboys made their own work songs, such as "The Old Chisholm Trail", driving the cattle and constantly adding new verses as they went, in a galloping rhythm.

"Git along little dogies" copied the rhythm of a gentler pace, to help along the motherless calves, or "doughguts", shortened to "dogies".

"Whoopee-ti-ti-yo, git along little dogies,
You know Wyoming will be your new home."

Night herding needed a soothing song, to prevent stampeding by cattle, or a bunch of nervous stage coach horses.

"Oh, slow up dogies, quit moving around,
You have wandered and trampled all over the ground;
Oh, graze along, dogies, and feed kinda slow,
And don't forever be on the go;
Move slow, little dogies, move slow."

A cowboy on the trail

The origins of this trail-song have been traced to an ancient Gaelic lullaby from western Ireland. Many work songs have been carried from one country to another, to cheer exile and keep fresh old memories. Such multiracial societies as Hawaii have had an influx from the east, especially Japan and Korea. So a Korean weaving song to beguile a long day's work is well known in Hawaii, and so is this rice-planting song from the Philippines. Sometimes it is performed with a dance. Often it is sung to the accompaniment of guitars, to speed up the monotonous group work of the stooping rice planters. They work in long rows, thrusting the rice seedlings into the mud, first to one side then the other.

> "Planting rice is never fun,
> Work from morn till set of sun,
> Cannot sit and cannot stand,
> Plant the seedlings all by hand."

Tedious shelling of dried peas was alleviated by refrains like "Oh de young girls so deceivin' ", and "Den lookoo wha' yo' do to me . . ." in a counting song from Trinidad.

Nomadic ex-convicts working in nineteenth-century Australia at the sheep shearing had their own work songs. An expert in those days before machines could clip a hundred sheep in a single day as he and his mates sang:

> "Click go the shear boys, click, click, click,
> Wide is his blow and his hands move quick."

Singing to sheep shearing in Australia

Just as any other folk songs, work songs were carried along in the singers' heads, wherever they travelled and adapted to new situations, new occupations.

Shanties

In essence, work songs are to lighten labour. Sea shanties were the work songs of sailing ship men, and the art died with the last of the British Cape Horners. But shanties have been recorded and collected from old sailors, who traditionally accompanied themselves on the concertina, accordion or fiddle, with the verses as unaccompanied solos. For reasons of superstition, shanties were only sung when working: on shore, sailors sang ballads and love songs.

Yet, of course, shanties borrowed from Negro slave songs and railroad work gang songs heard in ports, and mingled with them foreign words, just as folk songs did. The bulk of shanties came from West Indian seamen and from Irish Merchant Johns from Liverpool, New York, Ireland. Shantying had no audience, except in early passenger and emigrant ships. However enjoyable, it was practical music, demonstrating the saying: "A good song is worth ten men on a rope."

There is an early description of a pilgrim ship in 1400, sailing for the shrine of Saint James of Compostella, with the sailors shouting as they hauled a rope hand-over-hand. This "sing-out" eventually became a hauling song, such as this Scottish one recorded in 1549.

> "Heisa, heisa,
> Vorsa, vorsa
> Vou, vou,
> One long pull,
> More power
> Young blood,
> More mud."

Choruses of "Heave and ho, rumbelow" accompanied heaving the anchor, and calls like "Yo ho, heave ho!" "Rock 'n' Roll" was another common cry among shantymen. It was a shout of encouragement when hauling or heaving and came from the American Negro, just as Rock 'n' Roll dancing did.

> "Hoist her high an' hoist her dry, come rock 'n'
> roll me over,
> To me *way*, hay, hay, ho, *hu*!
> We're rolling down to Trinidad to meet Miss Lucyloo!"

In early days, a shantyman was of higher rank than ordinary seamen, and would sing solos to lead the men. Later on, an older hand with a powerful voice and a good memory would volunteer to be "the nightingale". Often he sang the chorus through first to let the gang know what shanty was coming, and started a verse with a cracking yell. In effect, he sang out orders and the labourers sang in response.

In the Royal Navy, early in the nineteenth century, fiddlers were included in the ship's company. A fiddler played for daily dancing of the hornpipe. This vigorous exercise kept the men's blood circulating well, and helped to prevent the disease scurvy. Larger ships had marine bands, but smaller ships kept on a fiddler and sailors took his jigs and reels, often Irish, his marches and waltzes, and made them into shanties.

There were many jobs: hoisting sails, pulling ropes and doing the walkaway stamps with them; there were long drags and short drags, and for each action there were different rhythms and songs.

A well-known old shanty, "Drunken Sailor", was sung in the sailing ships called Indiamen, its tune coming from a traditional Irish dance. The yell was: "Way hay" or "Way aye yah", or "Hooray".

The "hooraw" chorus accompanied the sending up of sails at

halyards, and was a stamp'n go, or walkaway song. Sailormen liked to pronounce early as "earl – eye".

"Way, hay an' up she rises!
Patent block o' different sizes,
Way hay 'n' up she rises
Earl – eye in the morning!
What shall we do wi' a drunken sailor . . .
Earl – eye in the morning?"

Hauling and heaving were easier, of course, when everyone pulled his weight. A song might also be used for pulling a boat up a slipway. The pull came on the last word of the chorus.

"Haul on the bowline, so early in the morning . . .
When I get back, I'll marry her in the morning . . .
And if she's married another man in the morning . . .
I'll black his eyes and I'm off to sea in the morning . . .
Haul away, haul, the bowline *haul*!"

Enthusiasts restoring old sailing ships have tried to revive the singing of shanties too. They still turn up. Apparently, when tackling odd corners which mechanical tools cannot reach, workmen in stone quarries in Portland use sea shanties. They sing in pairs, striking alternate blows, splitting the stones by metal wedges struck with their heavy mauls.

Street Cries

Not all work which inspired work songs was strenuous, except on the lungs perhaps.

As early as the fifteenth century, English traders brought their farm produce in from the country to the towns, and plied their

Street cries

wares in fairs, markets and crowded streets. Services, like sweeping chimneys, mending chairs, sharpening knives were also on offer. In time, special cries and rhymes developed. It was more appealing to sing out a rhyme, just as today, with the same cunning, television advertisers use sung jingles to promote their goods, knowing that catchy rhymes will be remembered.

We know of early English selling songs because many decorative engravings of the Cries of London and illustrated ballads still survive. Some of the songs were set to music by Elizabethan composers such as Orlando Gibbons (1583–1625) and Thomas Morley (1557–c.1603).

Side by side with young lambs, live eels, fresh spring water, brooms and pins, songs were sold for "Three yards a penny".

"Listen to my tunes so gay
And buy a ballad of me pray."

We retain today an affection for street markets and the hope of bargains. Singing trading was not great music, but it gave to dealing in a vast multiplicity of goods an attraction with which supermarkets selling just "everything" to the accompaniment of recorded music, cannot compare. For even the most raucous of traders were adding a sort of gaiety to their work with catches and songs.

American Negro Slave Songs

For any slave to sing may suggest a contradiction, but singing helped to lighten labour. Also it was a form of release for a race which seems to sing naturally, and with pleasure. Like shanties, slave work songs were narrated by a leader, who was accompanied by a chorus of "basers". They "spelled" him over while he took breath, singing their responses, or the next line, so that the humming and sounding of the music never seemed to stop, just like their repetitive work.

The accent fell on unstressed beats and produced the syncopation we know in jazz. Long notes were decorated with short notes called "trimmins". They cannot be written down, but you can hear them on records of Negro songs and religious "spirituals".

Again like shanties, Negro songs had shouts, and a treble quavering above the singers was claimed to make the "hair riz".

Shout songs were adapted for rowing, to keep the rhythm of the oars steady:

>"Knee-bone when I call you
>H – a – nn knee-bone . . .
>Knee-bone bend to the elbow bend."

Rice sheaves were thrashed on the floor by Negroes facing each other as they sang:

>"Peas an' the rice, peas an' the rice
>Peas an' the rice done done done done . . ."

Women and boys chanted as they beat the rice with pestle and mortar.

A woman churning butter would coax the milk:

>"Come budda come, Missus want e
>budda, come budda come . . ."

And scrubbing at the washboard or ironing, a woman might sing plaintively:

"By an' by – e I'm going t'see the King
Lord, I wouldn' mind dyin' if dyin' was all . . .
Wouldn' mind dyin' but I got t'go by myself . . ."

Hoeing in a cotton field made June a hard month, when the sun was hot and weeds grew fast.

"What y'u gwine t'do fo' June month?
Jerusalem Jerusalem
Pull off y'u coat an' go t'work – Jerusalem
Jerusalem
June month's a ha'd month – Jerusalem Jerusalem
. . . . . ."

Cotton picking

Black Prison Songs

Even today, when the work practices of nineteenth-century plantations have almost died out, the work songs, rooted in Africa, remain alive.

They are sometimes sung by black prisoners in southern prisons of the United States. The work leader shapes the lyrics to pace the jobs being done, to release at least the voice of the convict, even when his body is bound to drudgery. For though conditions have been greatly improved, prison work remains dull.

Rhythmic songs are used for cross cutting, when convicts hit with axes in turn to fell a large tree. Logging songs are for chopping wood. This axe song, with many verses, was recorded in a Texas prison in 1965.

> "Julie, hear me when I call you,
> Julie won't hear me
> JULIE WON'T HEAR ME.
> B'lieve I'll go to Dallas . . .
> Go to see my Julie
> OH MY LORDY."

Flat-weeding, or hoeing, might be done to this song:
"Oh my big-leg, bow-leg YELLOW YELLOW GAL . . .
Oh my knock-kneed, pigeon-toed YELLOW, YELLOW GAL . . .
Oh my yellow, my yellow, YELLOW YELLOW GAL . . ."

Cotton picking or sugar cane cutting has more solo songs, as the worker works on his own, has more breath to join in, to harmonize, to enjoy more complicated lyrics and tunes:

> "Oh it sure makes a man feel bad . . .
> Now if I had the governor like he had me . . .
> Wake up in the morning I'd set him free . . ."

The work song is dying now. Mechanization of work is making it obsolete. Men and women tending machines in factories lipread to talk to each other above the noise. Immigrant workers in England sometimes sing their own songs, but more often amplified records drown their voices as well as the machine's din. Remnants of work songs are still rediscovered by the explorations of diligent folk song collectors and performers. Then for a short while the work songs flicker to life again.

Slaves singing
as they cut cane sugar

13 Primitive Music

How CAN WE hope to know anything about primitive, prehistoric music? It is only by imagination we can hear the songs the cavemen sang, thousands of years before records were written. Or were they, in fact, too busy hunting for food, preparing it, eating it, making weapons or tools, and tending a fire for warmth and to keep wild beasts at bay? Did they sing at all? Did they chant stories and boast of exploits overcoming mammoth creatures as they rested in their caves in long evenings and freezing winters?

Cave painting

We do not know. Yet some cavemen practised an art of which they have left a record. Caves have been discovered with paintings and carvings of instruments which, being of perishable material, have rotted away long ago. In India, cave paintings and rock carvings show a wide variety of instruments.

Within the cave Les Trois Frères in south-west France is a scene which has been interpreted as a religious ceremony. A man disguised under a bison skin is holding a bow by his face, as if playing it, not shooting with it. As this work is dated by archaeologists as c.15,000 B.C. it suggests that Stone Age men did indeed have musical instruments. Archaeologists are not certain which came first, a bow for hunting, or a musical sounding bow, and if they developed independently.

A musical bow's string is tapped with sticks or stroked. If it is held near the open mouth, as in the cave painting, the vibrating string's sound can be changed by the mouth's movement, as in talking. For this changes the inside or cavity of the mouth as it acts as a resonator. One early rock painting in South Africa shows a bushman playing seven shooting bows as a musical instrument.

This technique is also used in the Jew's harp (see p. 28), still used for serenading in Austria, so many centuries later.

Having this clue about bows, we can suppose that primitive men also created noise makers, to scare away preying animals. What materials might they have used? First there was the ground. They might stamp with their feet, thump with their fists, bang with bones or sticks, drum at fallen trees. They might clang on stone slabs with rocks. Did they notice their caves echoing when they called to each other? Did they blow through animal bones?

Primitive men might have made ground bows in this way. A hole would be dug in the earth, and nearby a supple piece of wood put into the earth, with a string tied on its free end. The string was attached to a flat lid of bark or wood, put over the hole, and weighted down with stones or soil. The string was tightened until when plucked with a finger, it sounded.

More ambitiously, they might have made ground zithers. A hole in the earth, again used as a resonator, would be covered with a flat stone. Then a string would be braced up on a central stick standing on the stone, and other sticks bedded in the earth. This string would be played with tapping sticks.

The Music of Primitive Peoples Today

When we describe these early instruments, we have more than guesswork to guide us. They are actually played today. Primitive peoples, whose customs have remained virtually unchanged and undisturbed right up to this century, still use primitive sound makers. So Pygmies in the Congo make ground bows to pluck, and also have a second player to drum at the pit's cover. Children in Uganda use them as toys. Ground zithers are made in Uganda, in Indonesia and elsewhere.

The Aborigines of North Australia clack their boomerangs together, and play didgeridoos. These are drone pipes made from bamboo or hollow saplings, treated by soaking in water, then smeared with grease to improve the tone. They are about five feet long, though ceremonial ones can be ten or fifteen feet.

Scholars think it likely that bamboo was from the earliest times used to make musical instruments. Though such instruments would have disintegrated, their descendants can be heard in remote tribes of central Malaysia, or in Ethiopia, where one-note bamboo flutes are still played, with each player taking a turn to sound his individual note. Bamboo could also make drums, clackers, and, with skin stripped, string instruments.

It seems likely also that rattles and scrapers may have been made in prehistoric times. They too survive in tribal use, and are easily made, as noise makers or scarers, with seeds or stones to rattle in shells or gourds, and animal bones to rasp on stones or wood.

The music of ancient India, revealed in cave paintings and carvings of cymbals, clappers, castanets, bells, gongs, dancing rattles, drums, flutes, trumpets and other instruments, is known because these instruments are played today.

Musical instruments of India

Greek musician playing lyre.
In the background,
harp, lyre and cithara

Archaeological Evidence

From other early civilizations, such as Egypt, we have still more concrete evidence of musical instruments. Not only are there many representations of instruments in decorations and carvings, but actual instruments, such as primitive three-hole flutes, have been discovered by archaeologists in royal tombs. A more complicated form of frame rattle, the sistrum, has been found in the remains of ancient Egypt and Rome.

It is not only in tombs that actual instruments have been found. Occasionally they have been preserved in sand, like the sistrum and clappers illustrated. Peat bogs in Denmark and Ireland have yielded Stone Age trumpets; ice has kept bone flutes intact in Soviet Asia; ancient clay whistles have been excavated in Peru.

A miniature lyre (first called a harp), perhaps a replica, was found in the Sutton Hoo ship burial of the seventh century, in 1939. A reconstruction of this instrument has been made at the British Museum, and recorded accompanying the Anglo-Saxon poem *Beowulf*. The sound is piercing and metallic, like an unsoft harp.

For the ancient Greeks, the national instrument was a lyre, its strings plucked with a large plectrum in the player's right hand.

Lyres seem to have been used most for accompanying songs declaimed in a dramatic manner. From 2,000 B.C., simple flutes were heard more in the countryside than in the town, and the city musicians adopted short pipes of cane or wood, which had reeds in their mouthpieces. They accompanied singers with harps, and oddly were very often played in pairs. The Greek name was aulos, the Roman tibia.

Greek players also used a two-string lute they called a pandoura, and by 400 B.C. a trumpet playing competition was included in the Olympic Games.

Folk Instruments

There is other evidence about old musical practice in live folk music, which has been handed down by tradition and learnt by ear, repetition and imitation. Double piping, for example, is still seen today in the Mediterranean and Black Sea regions, with parallel pipes, sometimes joined together.

The hurdy gurdy was known in Europe before the tenth century, yet still is a folk instrument in central Europe. The strings are rubbed by a rosined wheel, which is turned by the right hand, while the left plays finger keys.

From the twelfth century, the pipe and tabor, sometimes with bagpipe as well, were popular for accompanying dancing. One man could play with his left hand a pipe, with two holes in front and one behind for his thumb, while drumming with his right hand. This old one-man-band survived to accompany Morris dancing early this century in England. It is still heard accompanying street dances called *farandoles* in Spain and Provence, with the dancers holding hands, sometimes threading their way through vineyards.

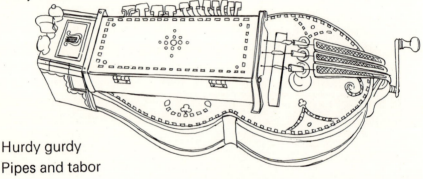

Hurdy gurdy
Pipes and tabor

Some early music groups, playing on old or reconstructed instruments, claim that old music has a special appeal today for those who enjoy folk and pop music just because it too has small groups, simple themes and an almost impromptu atmosphere.

Evidence from Documents

Early legends and documents also contribute to our knowledge of musical instruments. The invention of an instrument might be ascribed to a god. For instance, the Greek god Apollo was believed to have invented their cithara or lyre. Old documents in Chinese, Indian, Hebrew, Persian, Greek, Latin and Arabic describe music and its origins. Homer, Plato and Socrates all wrote about music in ancient Greece.

The Bible is a useful source of information, because it covers a long span of the history of the Hebrews, and describes instruments as well as the occasions when music was played.

In 1 Chronicles 25 there are long lists of musicians who served at King Solomon's court. Two hundred and eighty-eight musicians, playing harps, cymbals, psalteries, and singing performed at the dedication of his temple. When he married the Pharaoh's daughter, Egyptian instruments were introduced.

The story is well known of David, the shepherd boy, who was summoned to play to Saul, King of the Israelites, because David was known to be "a cunning player on the harp". "And it came to pass, when the evil spirit from God was upon Saul, that David took the harp and played with his hand; so Saul was refreshed, and was well and the evil spirit departed from him." (1 Samuel 16:23)

Origins of Instrumental Music

Even a brief outline shows that it is possible to piece together a fragmentary idea of ancient music. But we may still wonder how instrumental music came into being.

We can suppose that rhythm came in response to bodily movement, emphasizing or echoing work or play. It is perhaps most clearly seen when dancers click their fingers and the audience clap their hands in time to the dance, copying a rhythmic pattern which they first of all see.

Musicians in Uganda

The origin of melody is more difficult to attempt to trace. The human voice has many notes and tones in its range, and at first instruments may have copied these. For instance, a "speaking" slit drum for signalling, known in America and Africa, when beaten produces different notes, like a voice, because the slit which hollows out a tree trunk varies in width.

Players may have noticed that different instruments, played to reinforce rhythm, made sounds of differing quality. They may have combined the idea of percussion and tune in one "instrument", such as a set of tuned stone slabs, left in their natural site, nick-named rock gongs by explorers in Africa and Asia.

A similar instrument called a lithophone, with sixty stones, steel notes and bells as well, was played to Queen Victoria in 1848, and took thirteen years to assemble. One such instrument called the Till Rock Band toured in the United States and is now in a museum there.

These instruments represent an extraordinary recent rediscovery of what may have been noticed by fell climbers centuries earlier when they struck stones and heard clear notes.

In Africa there was an ancient form of xylophone which is still used in Uganda. Its bars are mounted on large banana stems, played by a group of players, sitting down, accompanied by drums.

This in itself represents a development which should be noted. Just as little children first play on their own, then by themselves alongside other children, then in real association with other children, so primitive players began by playing on their own. They may have taken turns to play, or played at the same time quite independently. Certainly some of the earliest instruments could be played as either melodic or percussion instruments. A musical bow was tapped to sound its note, but also tapped with seed shell rattles to make a toneless sound.

Playing in pairs or groups, as we know instrumental music, must have evolved slowly, for what mattered first to a player was that his instrument produced the sound he intended. So a tribal flute player, using a primitive instrument, sometimes supplies in a grunt those low notes which he cannot manage to sound in the rapid breathy tone of the flute. Listening to another player and combining with him was a long step forward.

14 Early European Music

Medieval musicians playing sacred music on a monochord, chimes, organ, harp, panpipes and cornett

Early Recorded Music

The church in Europe was an early and important patron of music. Music was used in church services, and sung and played by those who were the most educated of their period, those who could read and write. The Dark Ages which had gone before had left no records. During the ninth and tenth centuries, attempts to write down the melodies sung in services finally arrived at a simple form of recording music. This was in the first instance to record plainsong, which was originally an unadorned singing of the Latin words of the Mass, psalms and hymns, developed in the early centuries of the Christian church. It was almost like a chanted recitation, and needed no accompaniment.

St Augustine, sent in 597 by Pope Gregory to convert Britain to Christianity, sang with his followers a litany in unison. He was

Medieval musicians playing secular music on a
rebec, horn and drum

followed by teachers of plainsong. Organs may sometimes have
been used to keep singers in tune, but early ninth- and tenth-
century organs were primitive instruments, played by thumping
at the large keys. For many years, other instruments were regarded
with suspicion, as being from the "wicked" world.

Up to the tenth century, church music was only melodic. Gradually, it was elaborated by ornaments such as the melisma, when one
word or syllable was adorned with several notes. Different voices
began to rest on different notes at the end of a phrase, four or five
tones or whole-steps above or below, making rather hollow-
sounding "perfect" intervals. In time, chords made with thirds and
sixths as well as fourths and fifths came creeping in. Then the
plainsong was "held" by the tenor part, *canto fermo*, while the others
moved independently, singing different tunes.

This in essence was the beginning of polyphony, that is, combining several melodies into one piece. There were many experiments following the Norman Conquest in 1066, and much interchange of musicians and their music between England and France.

Plainsong and early church music can still be heard today in some Catholic churches and religious institutions. The tradition fostered in monasteries remains unbroken.

Secular Folk Music

Yet all the time, outside the walls of the great monasteries and churches, there was music. There had been, of course, music of the people, a folk music of song and dance, not composed by any one person, but evolved by frequent repetition, elaboration, being handed down by memory. It was a music unfettered by rules or restrictions. Yet the free rhythm of the early songs was a little like plainsong. Also it seems that melody came before instrumental music, which gradually began to accompany it.

Long before the Norman Conquest, the Anglo-Saxons had their own bridal songs, battle chants, and poems which were declaimed to rhythmic pluckings on the harp. The Anglo-Saxon gleeman or scop was an entertainer, who recited legends.

In Wales, the ancient harpists or bards sang genealogies, love and heroic ballads, in courts and elsewhere. The Welsh bards gathered at eisteddfodau from the seventh century onwards. Today there are still such meetings but the bards are concerned with the writing of poetry in Welsh.

Jugglers and Minstrels

Light entertainment in music was provided by troupes of musicians in company with acrobats, conjurors, bear-leaders and actors all over Europe. The name juggler comes from the Roman *joculator*, and soon was only given to the variety artist kind of musician. The Church often condemned the tumbling jugglers, but found the music of the more serious players irresistible, even though some sang complaints of abuses in the church and state. Household accounts of bishops from the thirteenth century record payments to visiting minstrels. They were in a sense early professional musicians: though some were humble wayfarers, others became attached to noble households.

When William the Conqueror invaded England in 1066 he had a minstrel as a personal attendant. This Taillefer was granted permission to strike the first blow and advanced singing, tossing his sword in the air and catching it, an old juggler's trick.

Edward IV (1442–83) employed thirteen minstrels, some part-time, and all instructed not to ask for tips. They played at meal-times and ceremonial occasions. During the fourteenth century, some minstrels formed "gilds", fraternities to protect their interests and good name, for instance to prevent amateurs from taking over their jobs. You may see a remnant of minstrels' life even today in old churches or large houses in England, where galleries were provided from which they could perform.

Minstrels and jugglers

Troubadours and Trouvères

Both these names mean finders or inventors. They were given to poet-composers who wrote poems to be sung, mainly in praise of women, but sometimes recording heroic deeds. The troubadours came from Provence in the south of France, and spoke that dialect, working from the end of the eleventh century to the beginning of the thirteenth. The trouvères, who spoke French, came from central and northern France, starting somewhat later than the troubadours.

Richard the Lion Heart (1157–99) was a noble troubadour, and records remain, noted as plainsong was, of songs he might have sung. Only the melody was ever given, and the singer would be expected to extemporize, make up his own accompaniment as he went along. Also it was expected that poems often would be sung, as Chaucer noted at the end of his *Troilus and Criseyde*, in 1385.

Troubadours reciting their poems

Waits

These musicians were watchmen, who sounded warnings or marked the passing of time, guarding buildings in the night and "sounding" at intervals with horns or other wind instruments.

Carols

Carols were rhyming songs sung in English, often with a repeated chorus. Originally they came from pagan dance songs. The church "borrowed" the well-known tunes, and set to them words teaching of Christ, and praising His mother and the saints. They were by no means only for Christmas time, but celebrated other seasons as well. And ballads, too, were sung, popular secular songs in the first place accompanying dances.

Mystery Plays

Mystery plays were performed, often out of doors, once a year in many towns and cities from the thirteenth century up to the Reformation, during the reign of Henry VIII (1509–47). They were dramatizations of Bible stories, intended to teach and interest the population, for whom they were a great delight, bringing to life such stories as Noah and the flood. Some plays used incidental music. Church musicians and their music, lay minstrels and their music, were both used, for instance, to help in the telling of the angel appearing to Mary, playing a harp, and the shepherds agreeing that the angels' music was more complicated than their own.

Processions

In medieval civic life processions too enlivened the streets, and would bring out the whole population to watch triumphal entries and state visits by kings and nobles. The church, especially in Italy and Spain, celebrated its feasts, such as Palm Sunday, with singing in procession, and bell-ringing.

From the reign of Henry I (1100–35) onwards, the King had his own choir of musicians, called the Chapel Royal, to sing mass in his court. This royal patronage provides information in its accounts, and later gave many opportunities to English composers.

Other Records

Richly illuminated manuscripts, such as the York Psalter (of the late twelfth century) picture musicians and their instruments.

Stained glass windows in churches dating from the fifteenth century often had angel musicians, in groups of nine, playing such instruments as the harp, psaltery, hurdy gurdy, an early bowed string instrument called the rebec, and the shawm, a double reed instrument from which the oboe developed. You will find carvings, too, in cathedrals.

In the Middle Ages, English embroidery was a thriving industry. Even in this we can find records of musical instruments, sewn trumpets, harps, chimebells, bagpipes, from the thirteenth and fourteenth centuries, on church hangings and vestments.

It is clear from even this brief outline that there are countless ways in which ancient and medieval music have left their traces to fascinate us today. They also inspire twentieth-century musicians to explore backwards into their past so that old sounds can be recreated and interpreted afresh.

In the court music of Japan direct descendants of players still

A collection of
old instruments

play music which is the same in essence as that which was played in the eighth century, the Gagaku, "noble and elegant music".

Western musicians today have been listening to such music from the east with its differing traditions. A Japanese composer has suggested that Japanese music grows vertically, like a tree, whereas western music proceeds horizontally. Yehudi Menuhin, the violinist, has improvised with the Indian sitar player, Ravi Shankar, learning from his apparently endless variations, the ragas. George Harrison, the former Beatle, has given a concert tour with Ravi Shankar in the United States, Messiaen (born 1908) has made use of Hindu drumming patterns in his compositions. East is meeting west, and the more we hear the voice of the old music the more are we able to accept it as music for us too, rather than as a bewildering, monotonous sound.

There is no rigid line between old and new. We can appreciate early music not only because it tells us how our modern music came into being, but for its own sake.

15 Styles and Composers in Their Times

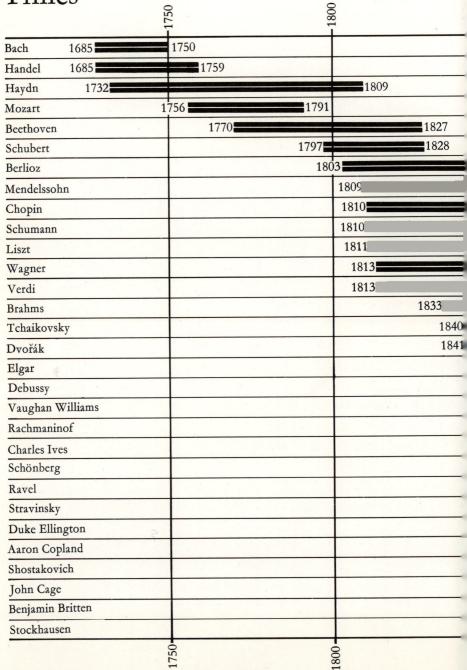

	1750	1800
Bach	1685 ▬▬▬ 1750	
Handel	1685 ▬▬▬▬ 1759	
Haydn	1732 ▬▬▬▬▬▬▬▬▬▬▬ 1809	
Mozart	1756 ▬▬▬▬ 1791	
Beethoven	1770 ▬▬▬▬▬▬▬▬▬▬ 1827	
Schubert	1797 ▬▬▬▬▬ 1828	
Berlioz	1803 ▬▬▬▬▬	
Mendelssohn	1809	
Chopin	1810	
Schumann	1810	
Liszt	1811	
Wagner	1813	
Verdi	1813	
Brahms	1833	
Tchaikovsky	1840	
Dvořák	1841	
Elgar		
Debussy		
Vaughan Williams		
Rachmaninof		
Charles Ives		
Schönberg		
Ravel		
Stravinsky		
Duke Ellington		
Aaron Copland		
Shostakovich		
John Cage		
Benjamin Britten		
Stockhausen		

Table of related lifespans of some composers
from Bach to Stravinsky

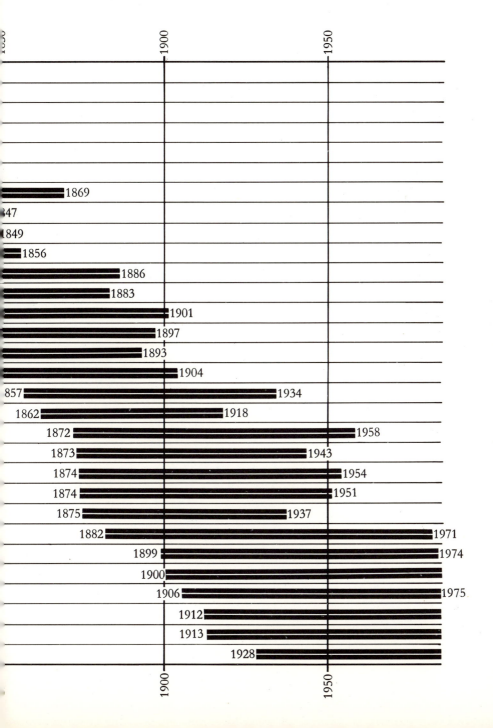

THE VOICE OF a composer is his own individual way of "speaking", expressing his musical thoughts. Some music is so individual that it is possible to recognize who the composer is after hearing only a few bars.

Other composers tend to belong more to a group of musicians who have developed a style of their own, and tried to bring it to perfection. Their music has strong similarities to that of their contemporaries: they are trying to write the same kind of music in the same way.

It is valuable to think about composers in the times they lived, even though, of course, they do *not* squeeze conveniently into neat pigeon holes or tidy centuries. Some have comfortably long lives, to mature their talents: others, like Mozart and Schubert, died tragically young, leaving us wishing for more.

To a certain extent every composer is influenced by his times, unless he deliberately adopts an imitation of an earlier style. For a composer makes up music quite simply in the forms and styles he has available, or can develop, and has been taught by listening to others or playing himself. And he writes for the instrumental forces which are available to him, suggesting and encouraging improvements, but, most probably, too busy writing music to invent new instruments as well.

So the introduction to composers, many of whom have full biographies written about their lives which you can consult later on, is grouped in centuries. This gives some idea of the way in which we have gradually come to inherit the wealth of music which is now, as never before, so easily available to us.

16 The Sixteenth Century

Forerunners

We do not know the names of the composers of much early music, for instance folk songs or plainsong. One of the most famous early English works was a round for six voices, "Sumer is icumen in", written probably late in the thirteenth century and apparently well ahead of its time in technique, but by a composer whose name is lost.

During the fourteenth century, names began to emerge, such as Guillaume de Machaut, a Frenchman (c.1300–77), who wrote Masses and secular songs too. In Italy, songs for two voices, often following each other "in imitation", were developed, using duple or triple time, that is, two or three beats in each bar. Sometimes they were accompanied by instruments; sometimes singing and dancing went together in the *Ballata*.

In England, the first major composer we know was John Dunstable (1370–1453) whose sacred and secular music was admired on the continent. He developed shapely melodic lines, and sometimes discarded the style of *canto fermo*, with the tune held by the tenor part. Having all the parts singing the same words tended to move the music towards the idea of chords, fully developed in the next century. Also there were experiments with sounding notes against each other which "clashed" briefly, or with the silence and rejoining of one voice into a piece of choral writing.

The sixteenth century saw the culmination of polyphonic writing in a sort of vocal orchestration, with the singing voices moving independently, or coming together in chords, or imitating fragments from each others' parts in groups or as soloists. The motet (unaccompanied sacred choral work) "Tu es Petrus", ("Thou art Peter"), by the Italian Palestrina (1524–94) is an outstanding example. And you can also listen to the works of the Spaniard Victoria (c.1535–1611), the English Byrd (1543–1623) and the Flemish Lassus (c.1530–94).

Madrigals

This term was given to an earlier song form, but in the sixteenth century was used for part songs, with the melody in the highest part, often accompanied by instruments. The first collection was published in Italy in 1533. After that there were five and six part settings of short poems, the words carefully set, and "illustrated" by the music.

Madrigal singing

The madrigal was taken up with enthusiasm by English composers. Listen to "The Silver Swan" by Orlando Gibbons (1583–1625). The music conveys perfectly the sadness of the swan's one and only song before her death. Also in England balletts (from the Italian *ballata*) were written for singing and dancing, in separate verses with "Fa-la" choruses, by Thomas Morley (1557–1603) and others.

The most famous collection of English madrigals was *The Triumphs of Oriana*. Based on an Italian model, twenty-nine madrigals were brought together to praise Queen Elizabeth I, each one ending "Long live fair Oriana".

The ayre seemed peculiarly an English form, which brought fame to John Dowland and the poet-composer Thomas Campion (1567–1620), who set his own poems as accompanied solos.

The Effect of the Reformation

The Protestant reformers, Cranmer in England, Luther in Germany and Calvin in Geneva, had one musical aim in common. They wanted their church congregations to have the service in their own languages, not Latin, and to take part in the singing with full understanding.

Martin Luther was a practical musician, and made clear that he did not intend "the Devil", that is secular music, to have all the best tunes. So he adapted them into Chorales (German hymns) and brought out the first Protestant hymn book in 1524. Also he borrowed from plainsong, and generally the effect was to simplify the style of music, and make composers think in terms of chords, blocks of notes (as in our hymn tunes), rather than melodies proceeding simultaneously.

The Development of Instrumental Music

Among the resources available to a sixteenth-century composer were church organs, sackbuts (trombones), shawms and pommers (ancestors of the oboe and bassoon), played in church or in the open air.

In the home or royal court were keyboard instruments, virginals, spinet, harpsichord and clavichord, the lute, recorders of various sizes and the viol family. The viols were flat-backed with six strings, and played either resting on the knees or between them. The tone was less bright than the violin, which eventually ousted them, becoming so much more popular.

Sets of viols were kept in chests, and during this century players would match up their parts to the written voice parts, and perform madrigals. We know this was common practice because some madrigals were presented as being "apt for voices or viols". And similarly, choral pieces were copied into the *Fitzwilliam Virginal Book*, another famous collection of pieces.

Gradually, however, composers came to realize that the use of repeated chords or running scales, so attractive in keyboard music, was not ideal for the voice or viols. They began to reconsider their style.

One form always played by instruments was the dance. Composers frequently paired a slow dance with a quick one; for example, a slow *pavane*, with two beats to the bar, then a quick *galliard* in triple time. This simple beginning eventually led to the more complicated forms the suite, sonata and symphony, developed in the next two centuries.

Another form to hand was the variation on a theme. This might have been a folk tune or a popular song of the sixteenth century, which the composer stated simply, then repeated with decorations on the tune, and varying accompaniments. This naturally fostered ingenuity in composers, and skill to demonstrate the characters of the instruments they chose.

The fantasia, or in English fancy, usually was a piece in descriptive style, illustrating, as the first kind of "programme music", such different happenings as the fall of a leaf, or a battle on a virginals' keyboard, or even a lute.

The greatest keyboard music of this period came from England. More than six hundred virginal pieces still exist, nearly a quarter by Byrd, and many are reprinted today, so that you can try them out for yourself.

In the sixteenth century, musicians began to combine instruments together deliberately, rather than combining them with or casually substituting them for voices. As the individual qualities of instruments emerged, so the music matched, with far-reaching influence on the composers who followed.

17 The Seventeenth Century

DURING THE COMMONWEALTH and Protectorate (1649–60) the Puritans made objection to what they considered over-elaborate church music. Secular music was still written and performed, and music clubs or "meetings" flourished in London, Oxford and Cambridge, some of them organized by out-of-work church musicians.

Oliver Cromwell had an orchestra of forty-eight violins to entertain his guests at his daughter's wedding, and took the organ from Magdalen College, Oxford, to his own palace at Hampton Court, for his private organist to play.

Charles II (1630–85) was restored to the throne of England in 1660, and processed up Whitehall to the sound of music for sackbuts and cornets by Matthew Locke. Perhaps then, on his thirtieth birthday, he was already planning a new place for Mr Locke, as composer for the violin in the King's Musick. In his exile, Charles had developed a passion for the violin, and a great delight in dance music, or any gay music to which he could beat time.

He set about restoring the Chapel Royal, disbanded under Cromwell's Protectorate, and, in imitation of King Louis of France, formed a band of twenty-four violins to play when he attended service. He sang bass, was proud of his keen ear, and laughed out loud if his choir at the Chapel Royal sang out of tune.

Gradually the violin came to take the place of the treble viol, although amateurs in particular continued to play the viols and older music. But the seventeenth century was a period of changes, and one of the most important was the emergence of professional virtuoso performers, on such instruments as the violin. This was brought about partly because under the Puritans there was less patronage from the church and nobility, so that many professional musicians made their living as teachers and public performers.

Public concerts were introduced in London by Banister, who was a Wait from St Giles-in-the-Field, in 1672, and then Thomas Britton in 1678, with great success, for thirty-six years. At first, Britton did not charge for his weekly concerts, but later a subscription of ten shillings a year was charged. Coffee was available at a penny a cup for the audience, who came to hear such performers as Handel playing a small organ or a virginal.

The diarist, Pepys, described as "mightily divertising" the

Spring (later Vauxhall) Pleasure Gardens in London, opened in 1660. Here people paid two shillings for popular concerts, but even more, five shillings, when there were firework displays.

Early Orchestras

During the seventeenth century, the orchestra began to have a standardized form recognizably like its modern counterpart. And for this grouping of instruments music was written in a truly instrumental style, not as for voices.

The instruments played by common musicians and waits in town bands included violins (fiddles), flutes, oboes, bassoons, trumpets, hunting horns and drums. It was these, and not the lutes and viols which had accompanied polyphonic vocal music in noble households, which made up the new orchestras. Instrument making was improved. The new violin's family came to be recognized as an effective orchestral foundation.

The playing of these mixed bands or early orchestras meant that there could be different combinations of tone above the harpsichord *continuo*, which played throughout, as if it were holding the piece together. Instead of music being woven in strands by voices, it progressed in harmonic groups of notes, thought of upwards from a "figured bass".

A group of instrumentalists

Such music was actually written down only as a bass line, with figures attached denoting the chords which the keyboard accompanist was to play, leaving him scope to "realise" and interpret his part as skilfully as he could, while the actual written notes were also duplicated by the bass viol, 'cello or double bass.

Figured bass was also called thoroughbass or *basso continuo*. This shorthand notation was used from about 1600 to nearly 1800, in violin sonatas, oratorios and Passions, works like Bach's Brandenburg Concertos, and for accompanying narrative or dramatic recitative in opera.

Bar lines were fixed. The various old modes retreated as the two main scales we know today, major and minor, were established.

Music with Drama

Operas, oratorios and cantatas were born early in the seventeenth century. They came into being in reaction against the old polyphonic style of music, in favour of a dramatic, declaimed style, intent on making the words clear. So they were accompanied by chords from the continuo, and made a sort of speaking music. However, the developing virtuoso voice demanded some scope, and was given the *aria*, to dwell on a melody and comment on the action, to express mood and feeling. Choruses returned to give

variety, and of course the old style polyphony persisted in church music as well as elsewhere.

What became clearer was a difference in the *styles* of music written for the church, for small-scale private or chamber music and for the theatre, something which was less evident in the sixteenth century.

SOME OUTSTANDING COMPOSERS

Claudio Monteverdi (1567–1643)

Monteverdi has a re-discovered voice, because recently his works have been revived and staged after many years of neglect. Some scores are lost, and others have to be "realized" from a figured bass. His rhythms are attractive and dancelike. Chords clash in harmony which sounds modern in its dissonance. He wrote in the old style, and in the new for operas, madrigals and masses, holding state and church positions, and finally dying in Venice.

His operas have dramatic and expressive music for the singers. In the earliest, *Orfeo* (1607), he apparently used all the forty instrumentalists available at the court of his patron, the Duke of Mantua. These included fifteen viols, two violins, flutes, trumpets, trombones, a harp, harpsichords and organs. This was in a way an experiment in early orchestration, and later he began to use the string orchestra as the main orchestral support.

Heinrich Schütz (1585–1672)

Schütz is sometimes given the nickname "the father of German music", because he seemed to foreshadow Bach and Handel. He visited Italy twice, was influenced by Monteverdi, and took home the Italian manner of using instruments independently from voices, not just doubling what they sang. His compositions, particularly his three settings of the Passion, show a straightforward simplicity and sincerity.

Jean Baptiste Lully (1632–87)

Lully left Italy, the country of his birth, for Paris, at the age of fourteen. By the time he was twenty, his skill at dancing and violin playing gained him a place in the service of King Louis XIV. He prospered, becoming court composer of dance music and court ballets, in which both he and the King sometimes took part. Lully combined with the playwright, Molière, in producing ballets and music for plays. His operas always included ballets; they used declaimed, well accompanied recitatives, and more choruses than Italian operas.

As an introduction which was more than an opening fanfare, Lully developed the "French" overture for his operas, a small suite of pieces in this order: a slow movement, played twice, a quick movement, then a moderately slow dance, or repeated section of the first movement.

The "Italian" overture had a quick, then a slow, then another quick movement. This form was sometimes called *sinfonia*, and was one of the ancestors of the works we call symphonies, sonatas and quartets.

Arcangelo Corelli (1653–1713)

Corelli is remembered as a founder of the great school of violin playing at Bologna, excelling as a performer, teacher and composer. With others, he composed many violin sonatas, church and chamber, this term describing, roughly, in seventeenth-century Italy a played piece, as cantata described a sung one.

Also he developed the *concerto grosso*. In this form, two contrasted groups of instruments play: one is the solo group, *concertino*. (Corelli used a string trio, two violins and 'cello.) The other, the *tutti* strings or *ripieni*, is a larger group. And the suite, a series of contrasting movements, mostly dances written in the same key, continued its development.

Alessandro Scarlatti (1660–1725)

Scarlatti was also an Italian, working mainly in Naples and Rome. He wrote more than a hundred operas, although many are lost, and about six hundred cantatas. His voice echoed in influence into the eighteenth century, when Italian opera was immensely popular in Europe.

François Couperin (1668–1733)

For over two hundred years, various Couperins were Parisian musicians, and François was called le Grand ("the Great") because of his special skill as a composer and performer on the harpsichord. He also served Louis XIV, as an organist.

He wrote dances, and many descriptive pieces with vivid titles, the music trying to convey a mood, describe a person or an event. Picturing something in sound is now called programme music.

Henry Purcell (1659–95)

Purcell lies buried in Westminster Abbey, London. He had been a pupil at the Chapel Royal, tuner of the Abbey's organ at fifteen, and at twenty the organist, later on a keeper and repairer of the King's wind instruments and also a court composer. We have little information about his private life: always he seemed to be called the "famous Mr Purcell", for he was much esteemed in his lifetime.

For us today, his genius seems to represent all the exciting progress which filled seventeenth-century music with life. Later English composers, such as Holst (1874–1934) and Britten (born 1913) have brought to our notice his originality and brilliance. (Listen to Britten's *Young Person's Guide to the Orchestra: Variations and Fugue on a Theme of Purcell*.)

Purcell wrote for the church, for court ceremonies and for the theatre, spanning English musical life. It has been said that his music is incapable of monotony. His dances are so full of rhythm that they seem to beg for accompanying movement. Often he carried the same rhythmic figure throughout a piece, which might be danced on stage, or used as music between acts of a play.

The theatre of his time was full of experiments. Songs and dances were immensely popular, and Purcell wrote incidental music to go with forty-four plays in a period of only six years. During his time, the orchestra was brought from the musicians' galleries, hidden away from the public eye, to its modern position in front of the stage.

Purcell's music deserved this prominence. Although he was often satisfying the desire for music to accompany stage spectacle in the popular masques of the day such as *Dioclesian* (1690), he produced brilliant solo, choral and instrumental writing, with strikingly bold dissonance, and dramatically telling use of voice and varied instruments. The English version of early opera was dominated by the idea that music accompanied pageantry as a sort of decoration. But if you listen to songs from Purcell's short opera with dancing, *Dido and Aeneas* (originally written for schoolgirls), you will realize that Purcell was a great dramatic composer, whose works can be revived today for far more than historical interest.

He is a festive composer, whose voice speaks with compelling attractiveness today. It is sad that he died too young to enter the great "classical" eighteenth century, which undoubtedly he would have graced.

The death of Dido
in Purcell's *Dido and Aeneas*

18 The Eighteenth Century

THE WORDS IN Genesis, "There were giants in the earth in those days" can well be applied to music in the eighteenth century. The first half of the century is dominated by Bach and Handel. Their work brought back polyphonic music to a new glory. Sadly, they never met, although Bach twice tried to arrange a meeting. During their time the fugue form (see p. 210) was perfected.

The great names of the second half of the century are Haydn and Mozart. They did meet, in 1781, and Haydn admired the work of the younger man, playing over his music with him and his father. Each learnt from the other, but neither could directly teach much to the fifth colossus of the century, Ludwig van Beethoven. Beethoven had a few lessons with Mozart, and some rather unsuccessful teaching from Haydn, but he was in a sense stretching forward, away from them, to express his own genius in an individual style, which fitted the mood of the nineteenth century, into which he lived for many working years.

In the later part of the eighteenth century, the classical sonata, string trio and quartet, and the symphony were all developed to a high peak of excellence. By the time Beethoven began to use the orchestra, its form was standard, based on the strings of the violin family. The harpsichord continuo part was sometimes discarded. The improved pianoforte began to take the place of the harpsichord and clavichord as a solo instrument.

SOME OUTSTANDING COMPOSERS

Antonio Vivaldi (c.1677–1741)
Bach was influenced by Vivaldi's prolific writing, and rearranged and copied out some of his works for interest. Vivaldi wrote many *concerti grossi* (see p. 212). As a violinist, he wrote very sympathetically for strings. Listen to *The Seasons*, a set of four short violin concertos, each in three movements, fast, slow then fast.

Domenico Scarlatti (1685–1757)
The son of Alessandro Scarlatti, Domenico is best remembered for his harpsichord writing, and brilliant performance on that instrument. Once, when they both were twenty-three, he competed

with Handel, and they were judged equal. Domenico also composed church music, and spent many years in Spain, but his voice, as that of Liszt on the piano in the next century, is that of a virtuoso composer performer.

Johann Sebastian Bach (1685–1750)

Bach's life was a quiet one, dedicated to music. He came from a musical family, married twice and had twenty children, several of whom were noteworthy musicians. His life was spent entirely in Germany, in service to the church or a prince's court, and the work he wrote was dictated by his appointments and his own musical conscience. Although he produced a great deal of music, he was revered most in his lifetime for his skill as an organist and extemporist. After his death, his music was almost forgotten until Mendelssohn with others brought it to light again, beginning with a centenary performance of the St Matthew Passion in 1829.

Bach studied and copied Italian and French music, but used them to bring the German contrapuntal style in which he had been

J. S. Bach

brought up, to an unsurpassed level. He towers in the history of music because of this, and it is well illustrated by his development of the fugue. This, in essence, is a piece in which melodic parts or threads called voices introduce in turn a scrap of music called the subject. Then they play around with it, and a countersubject may be introduced. The voices interweave, echo and answer each other, may pass through many keys and changes, but do not "forget" the original subject, which is usually re-stated at the end of the fugue by each voice.

Bach used this form with infinite variety, and you may have heard some of his Forty-Eight Preludes and Fugues, *The Well-tempered Clavier*, celebrating an improved system of tuning. *The Art of the Fugue* is an unfinished work which demonstrated in music Bach's technical skill, a matchless manifesto.

His life can be divided into three main spheres of activity. He started as an organist. As a young man, he took long walks to hear famous organists. In 1708, he was made court organist to the Duke of Weimar. Later he wrote many cantatas for the chapel, as concert master.

Then from 1717 to 1723 Bach concentrated on instrumental music, suites, concertos and sonatas performed by his new master, Prince Leopold, at Cöthen. Here were written the six great Brandenburg Concertos, deservedly the most admired pieces in *concerto grosso* form.

In Leipzig, from 1723, Bach took a post at St Thomas's Church, and worked there ceaselessly until his death, having to produce and perform more than fifty cantatas each year, yet also composing his greatest choral works, the St Matthew Passion and the Mass in B minor, with many others.

Bach visited Frederic the Great at Potsdam in 1747, and composed for him a "Musical Offering" of pieces based on a subject given by the King. But this was an isolated event, and Bach more often worked almost in obscurity, certainly humbly, considering the depth of his genius.

His voice is that of a convinced musician and a devout Christian. His music seems full of serenity. It is touching to think that, though the contrapuntal style was soon to be considered too complex and learned, Mozart kept by him, to play for inspiration, Bach's preludes and fugues.

Handel in London

George Frederic Handel (1685–1759)

When Haydn heard Handel's oratorio *The Messiah* in Westminster Abbey, where he is buried, he wept and declared: "He is the master of us all." Handel's voice is masterful and magnificent. His music is solidly dignified.

In spite of parental opposition, Handel decided to be a musician, was a violinist in the opera orchestra at Hamburg, then visited Italy, where he was well received as a harpsichordist and organist. This Italian influence affected his whole life. When he returned to Germany, and in 1710 became director of music to the Elector of Hanover, later George I of England, he wrote many operas in the Italian style. Handel was a widely travelled bachelor, and often worked freelance in the expensive theatre productions which dominated his musical life until about 1740.

From 1712, Handel had taken up residence in England, and was admired and fêted. However, in 1728 *The Beggar's Opera* by John Gay introduced to London the "ballad opera". It was full of popular songs instead of Italianate arias, and had spoken dialogue in English based on everyday life instead of historical myths, as in

Italian opera. This swing in popularity made Handel decide to leave opera, and concentrate instead on oratorio, with much splendid choral writing which is still often performed today. Also he composed church anthems and organ concertos.

Throughout his life, Handel was a public musician, ever conscious of what would please his audience, whether it was the King of England enjoying water music on the river Thames, played from an accompanying barge, or twelve thousand people at the Vauxhall Pleasure Gardens, hearing from the then giant orchestra of one hundred the final rehearsal of short pieces to be played at a royal firework display.

Joseph Haydn (1732–1809)

Haydn was born into a humble Austrian family, went to choir school at six, then became a chorister at the cathedral of Vienna. There he heard the sonatas and symphonies of Carl Philipp Emanuel Bach (1714–88), Bach's fifth child, and modelled his early compositions on them. In fact, Mozart said of C. P. E. Bach: "He is the parent and we are the children." He wrote seventy sonatas for harpsichord or for harpsichord with one or two violins and 'cello.

Haydn became musical director to the Hungarian Esterházy family, and in that post had security, and an orchestra and singers at his command to write for performance in the chapel, theatre or palace court room. When he visited England, he was very popular, conducting his "Salamon Symphonies" from the keyboard. Late in life he wrote the oratorios *The Creation* and *The Seasons*, remembering his admiration for Handel's works.

The nickname "father of the symphony and string quartet" is given to Haydn because, in more than a hundred symphonies, he transformed the symphony from a work in a light "gallant" style to music whose effect came from the use of strong form or pattern. This emphasis is sometimes called *classical*. The orchestra advanced to complement what became an independent orchestral piece in three movements, quick, slow, then quick again.

Similarly, the sonata originally had three movements, all in one key. Then differing keys were used, and sometimes Haydn and Mozart used the dance, a minuet, to make up the second or third movement.

In the string quartet and quintet, beginning the idea of what we now call chamber music, the four or five instruments (see p. 52) played as equals in importance what were really miniature sonatas or symphonies.

Throughout his long life Haydn's voice as a composer was that of a hard-working and good-humoured craftsman, usually accepting his position philosophically, and using it to the best advantage.

Wolfgang Amadeus Mozart (1756–91)

At the age of three, Mozart became interested in his older sister Nannerl's lessons on the clavier. He began to compose and his father, Leopold, a violin teacher, realized that he was a prodigy and took him with his sister on a performing tour, to courts and monasteries. Their success was immediate, and overwhelming. Only writing numbers and sums seemed to fascinate Mozart as much as music.

Leopold then took them to Paris and in 1764, to London for a year. Wolfgang was received warmly by King George III and his Queen as a "Wunderkind" ("Wonder-child"). Also he met and played with "the English Bach", Bach's son Johann Christian Bach (1735–82), who was music master to the King's family, and was writing in the Italian style. In 1769, Mozart went to Italy, and, of course, heard a great deal there. Although welcomed, he was not offered an appointment which would have kept him there, bettering his early attempts at Italian opera.

It was difficult to settle in Salzburg in the service of the Prince Archbishop, treated as one of his servants, even though Mozart did manage to take a tour in France. His music was light, luxuriant in the "gallant" style, rather in contrast with his actual life.

Then in 1781, he left for Vienna, and presented himself as a virtuoso on the harpsichord, taught the piano, and produced many concertos, and other piano pieces.

As a token of his admiration for Haydn, Mozart wrote six string quartets. Then, in turn, Haydn was influenced by Mozart's work, and in all wrote eighty-three quartets. Mozart composed other chamber music, including the famous Clarinet Quintet, and many violin sonatas, nearly fifty symphonies and nearly twenty operas and operettas.

The major contribution of such masterpieces as the operas *The Magic Flute* and *The Marriage of Figaro* was that the characters were almost for the first time living creatures, whose music described and suited them perfectly. The operas were successful in his lifetime, but the gaiety of much of Mozart's music was not matched in his life. He was never a good manager, and he was frequently in debt during the last years of his life. The strenuous tours of his childhood may have undermined his health. The young man who had loved to dance, and wrote hundreds of entertaining letters to his family and friends, became depressed by his struggles to make enough money, and fearful of an early death. Some people detect a despairing undercurrent in his music. Certainly it is never lightweight.

An extraordinary quality of his talent was that he composed in his head, and could do the actual writing down in a crowded room. He described the inventing as a sort of "lively dream", hearing all

Mozart

the musical parts at once. He even said, when ill, that composing tired him less than resting.

It was tragic that Mozart did not find a congenial secure job, did not settle in England, where he might have found one, but struggled to make ends meet while his music poured out until he died at the age of thirty-five.

It seems that he was effortlessly gifted in music, and his voice, for many, is still as for those who heard him as a child, miraculous.

Handel, Bach, Haydn and Mozart well represent the eighteenth century, which was a time when the *form* of music was specially important, either being established or carried to perfection. Many composers lived under discipline too themselves, in service to churches or court, and producing work to order. Some were irked by living as servants, wearing livery like them, and in the next century there is a marked change in the way in which composers were employed, or earned a living.

19 The Nineteenth Century

THE NINETEENTH CENTURY is full of individual voices. Beethoven, one of the most individual composers ever to have lived, bestrides the transition from Classical to Romantic, from the eighteenth to the nineteenth century. In a sense, he belongs to both. His works were a pinnacle of the use of classical forms, such as the symphony. His temperament, aspirations and attitudes were Romantic in their intensity.

The Romantic composer tended to compose to express himself as an artist, without undue curbs of form or other discipline. The system of patronage was beginning to break down and the composer began to be a freelance. He no longer necessarily wrote music for a useful purpose. He no longer wrote it when he was told to do so by his employer. Of course, wealthy people still supported musicians with money and opportunities for performance, and Beethoven, for instance, dedicated works to Prince Karl Lichowsky. But he wrote what he wished, which his audience could take or leave, as they pleased.

This freedom was matched by similar experiments in art and literature. The nineteenth-century Romantics found strong links between music and literature. Programme music, depicting a story, or even a mood, demanded a new loosening of form. Music was used to illustrate, and to express strong feelings, without the bonds of a set form.

As music was now not just a "job of work" but an art, musicians such as Berlioz, Schumann, Liszt and Wagner all wrote to theorize about it, and to explain their ideas to the general public.

Almost taking the place of appreciation of form or shape, the enjoyment of pure sound in its own right came to have a high priority. Wagner and Debussy each interpreted this preoccupation differently and characteristically.

In essence, old limits were no longer accepted. Music became almost as diverse as the nationalities of its composers.

SOME OUTSTANDING COMPOSERS

Ludwig van Beethoven (1770–1827)

Beethoven's voice gathered all the authority of eighteenth-century classical composers, then, with increasing confidence, spoke for himself in a unique tone, which reverberated in influence right through the nineteenth century to Brahms, who died in 1897.

Beethoven was born into a poor family. His father was a singer, in service to the Elector of Cologne at Bonn, and Ludwig's first job as a boy was as assistant orchestral harpsichordist, and conductor from the keyboard. But at twenty-two, he settled permanently in Vienna, as a freelance pianist and composer.

In his early work, even though he used Haydn's and Mozart's works as models, his own manner began to emerge: strong emotion was openly evident in slow movements, and forceful, sudden changes of style in a way to suit himself rather than to fit any strict pattern. His manuscripts and sketch books demonstrate that he did not compose with ease. The struggle to express exactly what he wanted to be heard was marked by many corrections.

The second period continued to carry forward and extend what Haydn and Mozart had done. The Third to the Eighth symphonies

Beethoven

were written, piano sonatas, the Violin Concerto, some string quartets, and his one opera, *Fidelio* (1805), considered a masterpiece. He was using more changes of keys, making movements longer, and joins between them almost imperceptible. Beethoven found for his first symphony (performed in 1800) a standardized orchestra, based on strings, with wind instruments giving changes of tone "colour". By his Fifth Symphony, Beethoven had brought more instruments into the orchestra, such as the piccolo, double bassoon, and three trombones. Listening to all the symphonies, you witness a progress of immense musical energy.

From the age of thirty, Beethoven began to lose his hearing, and was completely deaf in the last years of his life. Although this must have been an agonizing loss, which caused devastating loneliness, Beethoven's compositions were in no way diminished. He produced the giant, dramatic Choral Symphony, his ninth, its last movement a choral setting of Schiller's "Ode to Joy" for four soloists, chorus and orchestra.

His music seemed to develop from small themes, to "grow" of its own accord, no longer always needing the supporting framework of the earlier rigid forms. So, for instance, in his late string quartets he wrote music which many at first considered impossibly difficult to play or "understand".

Yet Beethoven's inner ear informed him correctly that he had made a music which, though new and adventurous, was much more than that. The late string quartets represent a triumph not only of determination, but of an artist who in enforced intense meditation had moved from music expressing feeling to music expressing thoughts equally well.

Robert Schumann (1810–56)

Schumann married an accomplished pianist, Clara Wieck. He had struggled against her father's opposition, and in their first year of marriage wrote over a hundred songs. He wrote a great deal of piano music and chamber music, a piano concerto and four symphonies before he died at forty-six.

Also he is remembered for the considerable influence he exerted by founding the *New Journal for Music*, intending to encourage the poetic voice in music, and bring musicians' work to public attention, including that of Chopin.

Schubert and his song "Der Erlkönig"

Franz Peter Seraph Schubert (1797–1828)

Although Schubert never ventured to introduce himself, in 1827 a friend did show some of his songs to Beethoven, who was said to praise them. Later that year, in March, Schubert and two friends visited the dying Beethoven.

Schubert was one of the thirty-six torch bearers at Beethoven's funeral, and only lived one year longer. His friends were less aristocratic than Beethoven's supporters. He came from a musical family, a schoolmaster's son, and lived simply within a circle of friends, some of them poets and painters, who first heard his songs and encouraged him.

Schubert's pleasure was in composition. "I live and compose like a god." He was poor. His wealth lay in the astonishing ease with which he produced melody. His tunes seem to flow spontaneously. He is famed as a song-writer, and it seems that his themes sang through all his works, symphonies, sonatas and string quartets. He has been criticized for having limited grasp of form in his music. It is sad that he did not live long enough to attempt work in opera. His one oratorio, *Lazarus* (1820), was unfinished.

Listen to his "Trout" piano Quintet to hear how Schubert used one of his own songs as a theme in a ravishingly attractive chamber work.

Hector Berlioz (1803–69)

The Frenchman, Berlioz, was a friend of Romantic writers such as Hugo and Balzac, the painter Delacroix, the musicians Chopin and Liszt. His declared attitude to his work was essentially Romantic: "not rule, but direct reaction to feeling". In his life, he had many loves. In his music, he was intent on expressing the feelings of poets such as Shakespeare, Scott and Goethe. Not only poetic works but events were used to arouse emotions, and provide "programmes" to symphonic music, such as the *Fantastic Symphony*. This he bound together by the use of an *idée fixe*, a recurring theme.

He attached great importance to the tone "colour" of his music, sometimes demanding vast forces, huge choirs and orchestras, yet being capable of delicate work too. He wrote a great deal about music, most valuably on orchestration in the enlarged orchestra.

Felix Mendelssohn-Bartholdy (1809–47)

Mendelssohn used his influence to found a conservatory, or school of music, at Leipzig, and to conduct the series of Gewand-haus Concerts there.

He was born into a wealthy family. His talent was recognized early, and he had written fifteen symphonies and an opera before he was fifteen years old! This fluency has caused him to be considered at times a shallow composer. But he used the classical forms with great craftsmanship, and brought to them Romantically lyrical themes and an immediately appealing use of the instruments of the orchestra.

His music, such as the "Italian" Symphony, and the *Fingal's Cave* concert-overture (written as an independent piece), is delightful and charming. Not surprisingly, he was well liked in England, and played the piano for Queen Victoria and her German husband, Prince Albert, when he visited them in 1842.

Johannes Brahms (1833–97)

When Brahms was twenty, Schumann wrote that he "would bring us mastery". He claimed that the younger man's playing made of the piano "an orchestra of lamenting and exultant voices". This was the Romantic side of Brahms' talent, but he was also Beethoven's successor in that he gave a firm structure to his works, still using the classical forms of symphony, concerto and quartet.

In fact, he modestly held back the first of his four symphonies until he was in his forties, conscious of Beethoven's giant shadow. Also critics of the time insisted on contrasting him with Wagner, whose talent was dramatic. Brahms was not forceful like Beethoven, nor dramatic in an operatic sense, but purposeful in his writing, more considered than impulsive.

His chamber music is full of songlike beauty, and the lyrical line of his work is all important. It seems that his melodies are curved, rounded. Listen to his Clarinet Quintet, and *Four Serious Songs*.

In Brahms' piano and violin music, there are traces of Hungarian dances. Early in his career, he played in cafés and dance halls, and toured with a Hungarian violinist. He was also friendly with Joachim (1831–1907), another Hungarian violinist who played under Mendelssohn and Liszt, and founded a famous string quartet. Brahms was a bachelor, and valued this friendship especially, as also his association with the Schumanns.

César Franck (1822–90)

César Franck lived and taught so long in France that it is often forgotten that he was born in Belgium. His Symphony in D minor and Symphonic Variations are popular concert pieces today.

Anton Bruckner (1824–96), Gustav Mahler (1860–1911), and Richard Strauss (1864–1949)

These three are Romantic composers, influenced by Wagner. *The Song of the Earth* gives the flavour of Mahler's music, the large-scale orchestration, the rich colour of instruments. The works of Richard Strauss are lusciously orchestrated in apparently never-ending phrases, full blown with emotion, as you can hear in his opera *Der Rosenkavalier*. His symphonic poem *Till Eulenspiegel's Merry Tricks* is a popular concert piece.

Bruckner was both Classical and Romantic in tendency. He wrote nine symphonies as Beethoven did, and admired and was influenced by Wagner's music.

VIRTUOSO COMPOSERS

Frédéric Chopin (1810–49)

Chopin was Polish, but lived almost half his life in Paris, enjoying the company of the Hungarian, Liszt, and the Italian opera composer, Bellini (1801–35). From him, Chopin learnt to make the piano "sing", giving shapely lyrical melodies to his fingers in the same way that opera singers sang with grateful pleasure Bellini's arias. Chopin is often called "the poet of the piano" because of this, and the way he could convey even moods and feelings, in a fashion not attempted before. His own performing life began at nine.

Almost all his work was for the piano and included preludes, lively mazurkas and polonaises, and beautiful nocturnes, which he performed to adoring audiences until his early death at thirty-nine. Mozart's Requiem was played before four thousand people at his funeral. Chopin had said: "Play Mozart in memory of me and I will hear you," an intriguing link with the eighteenth century.

Serge Rachmaninof (1873–1943)

In his lifetime, Rachmaninof was famous as a conductor and pianist, touring a great deal. Today, his best known works are his three piano concertos, and the *Rhapsody on a Theme of Paganini*, written in 1934.

This piece is interesting because in addition, the theme had been given a set of variations by Paganini, and by Brahms. Schumann had used it, and so had Liszt.

Niccolo Paganini (1782–1840)

Although he did compose violin music, the Italian Paganini's phenomenal mastery as a performer was so great that legends grew up that he was in league with the devil. Crowds struggled to touch him to prove that he was human.

When Liszt heard him in Paris, in 1831, he decided to work to achieve equal virtuosity in his piano playing. He spent twenty years polishing a set of *Études* (studies), inspired both by Paganini himself and his *Caprices*, finally dedicating them to Schumann's wife, Clara. The technical demands are still a stimulating challenge to performers today. Listen to Alfred Brendel's recording.

Chopin

Franz Liszt (1811–86)

Liszt was a virtuoso pianist, achieving a brilliance which astounded and enthralled Europe. He was praised by Beethoven at the age of eleven, in Vienna, before triumphs in Paris.

As a teacher, he encouraged and championed many young musicians, such as Grieg, Wagner (who became his son-in-law), and Berlioz, conducting their works. Many of his own compositions were "transcriptions", or arrangements for the piano, but also he is considered to have invented the symphonic poem. This is a kind of programme music in which the form varies according to the subject, and is, of course, much freer than in a symphony. He used the device Metamorphosis of theme, so that a theme could change to match the literary scheme or idea of the piece.

OPERATIC COMPOSERS IN THE NINETEENTH CENTURY

Richard Wagner (1813–83)

Wagner was a great innovator, who slowly developed a new form of opera which he called music drama. Except for the beautiful *Siegfried's Idyll*, nearly all his best work was for the stage, with which

Wagner and a scene from *Siegfried*

he was familiar from a childhood in a theatrical family.

He wrote at length to describe what he aimed to do, which was to make the dramatic action just as important as the music. So gradually he evolved a continuous musical tapestry, not in set lengths, but in lyric melodies or recitatives as the libretto required, with the orchestra embroidering a surrounding web of sound. He enlarged the orchestra, and made it comment on the action with musical illustrations. In particular, the *leitmotiv* ("leading theme") linked characters, places or moods with a particular scrap of music, which was repeated or developed as the drama unfolded, helping to give it unity.

Also Wagner's harmony was new, using, as Liszt had done too, "modern" sounding chords with other notes added from different keys, roughly speaking, *chromatic* chords. (The chromatic scale includes all the semitones, all the black and white notes if you play from C to C on the piano.)

Wagner wrote his own libretti, usually basing them on old German legends. He supervised in detail the productions of his operas, such as the four dramas making up *The Ring* and *The Mastersingers*, in the little theatre at Bayreuth, where his works are performed in annual festivals today. This theatre, completed in 1876, was made possible by Ludwig II of Bavaria, who supported Wagner, after many years of financial and political difficulties.

Wagner's singers need heroic voices. The prevailing tone of his operas is rich: it is not surprising that he liked to surround himself with curved, swathed furniture, and stroked silken material for inspiration while he inhaled perfume sent specially from Paris.

Giuseppe Verdi (1813–1901)

Supporters of Wagner attacked Verdi, for he represented the traditional in opera. He developed the work of his fellow Italians, Bellini and Donizetti (1797–1848), deepening the dramatic importance of the characters, whom he tried to bring alive by his music. In his last years, Verdi also made some use of *leitmotiv* in *Othello* and *Falstaff*.

These Grand Operas, such as *Rigoletto* and *La Traviata*, are greatly enjoyed today for their supreme achievement in providing long of the utmost splendour for the human voice.

Other Notable Operas

Other notable operas were Rossini's *The Barber of Seville* (1816) and *William Tell* (1829). In 1863 and 1899 came the two parts of *The Trojans* by Berlioz. Then there were Smetana's *The Bartered Bride* (1866); Johann Strauss's *Die Fledermaus* (1874); Bizet's *Carmen* (1875); Borodin's *Prince Igor* (1890); Humperdinck's *Hansel and Gretel* (1893) and Puccini's *La Bohème* (1896).

Later on in 1902 came Debussy's *Pelléas and Mélisande* in 1904, Puccini's *Madame Butterfly* and in 1911 Richard Strauss's *Der Rosenkavalier*.

When you have the opportunity to hear or see a full performance of any of these, you will find it a rewarding experience.

SOME NATIONALIST COMPOSERS

Often composers are called nationalist if they make deliberate use of the folk music of their own country. But during the nineteenth century, many composers seemed to write rather in a style which revealed the inborn feeling of their own country, in reaction, perhaps, against the idea that Germany alone could produce great music and musical development, as she had done throughout the eighteenth century. They voiced the musical language of their native lands.

Glinka (1804–57) led the Russian "school", followed by Mussorgsky (1839–81), Rimsky-Korsakov (1844–1908) and, expressing his Russian music emotionally, Tchaikovsky (1840–93). (See also ballet music, pp. 205–6). Listen to his Sixth Symphony, the "Pathétique". Though not deliberately Finnish in use of material, Sibelius (1865–1957) has been called nationalist in sentiment in a similar way. Smetana (1824–84) and Dvořák (1841–1904) wrote from their native Bohemia, Granados (1867–1916) and Manuel de Falla (1876–1946) from Spain. Kodály (1882–1967) and Bartók (1881–1945), who has written a great deal for children, and collected nearly seven thousand folk tunes, drew much from their native Hungary, writing on into the next century. You will know the Norwegian Grieg's music (1843–1907), such as the *Peer Gynt* suites, and the Piano Concerto, also the Viennese waltzes of the two Johann Strausses, father and son (1804–49, and 1825–99).

In England, Gilbert and Sullivan produced their entertaining operas between 1875 and 1896. Parry (1848–1918), best known perhaps now for his setting of Blake's "Jerusalem", wrote very English sounding, firm textured choral music. Vaughan Williams and Gustav Holst used English folk music for inspiration.

Edward Elgar (1857–1934), living across the two centuries, conveys in his music an Englishness which is idealistic, with noble tunes which seem to enshrine a golden era of warmth and beauty.

SOME IMPRESSIONIST COMPOSERS ACROSS 1900

Claude Debussy (1862–1918)

In painting, the impressionists such as Monet and Turner, in poetry Verlaine and Mallarmé, had as their priority the art of *suggestion*. Debussy's music is similarly atmospheric. It is restrained, but not formal in the classical sense. The feelings expressed are hinted at rather than declared Romantically or dramatically.

Debussy is concerned in a new and individual way with expressing a mood in sounds, by means of subtle orchestration. He experimented with clusters of notes instead of traditional chords which "led" to others, or "resolved". Listen to his tone poem, *Prélude à l'Après-midi d'un Faune*, used as a ballet-score; *La Mer*, a musical account scored for a large orchestra, and his piano music, such as the "Golliwog's Cake-Walk", from the *Children's Corner Suite*.

Frederick Delius (1862–1934)

Delius was born in England, but spent a great deal of his life abroad. His music is luscious in its orchestration. The impression is of the composer enjoying the rich blend of sounds he conjures up in a highly personal, chromatic style, immediately recognizable in *On Hearing the First Cuckoo in Spring* or *The Walk to the Paradise Gardens*.

Maurice Ravel (1875–1937)

As a pupil of the composer Gabriel Fauré (1845–1924), Ravel was taught to admire classical form, and, though influenced by impressionism, wrote in a less fluid style than Debussy. His technique in piano and orchestral composition also brought new sounds to be enjoyed for their own sake.

Some of his most attractive pieces are the dreamy *Pavane for a Dead Infanta*, the *Bolero*, building up to a ferocious climax (also used for ballet), and *Le Tombeau de Couperin*, an orchestral suite.

The nineteenth century spills over with talent. Composers revered their predecessors from the eighteenth century, met each other in person, became each other's supporters, travelled extensively, performed to large audiences. The buds of talent which blossomed into music we consider characteristic of the twentieth century were well established at the turn of the century. Music opened out into a myriad blooms. (Look at the chart, pp. 144–5). For instance, by 1900 Elgar was already forty-three, Vaughan Williams twenty-eight, Stravinsky eighteen, and the ragtime composer, Scott Joplin, thirty-two.

20 The Twentieth Century

MUSIC IN THE nineteenth century was diverse. In the twentieth century it is complex as well. Within this relatively short span, there have been experiments which at first seemed outrageous, but were capped by others which seemed to be experiments for their own sake rather than to produce music as it had been understood in earlier times.

As in, for example, transport, the *pace* of change has been startling. Old-established, well-tried systems have been jettisoned. Sometimes the struggle to be different and new has produced a non-music, masquerading with great seriousness while audiences are puzzled, or walk out disappointed.

It has always been difficult to recognize what is valuable and lasting in "avant-garde", experimental music of your own time. Critics' mistakes, condemning strange new works, are gleefully quoted years later, when the pieces are accepted as classics. A critic wrote: ". . . poor Beethoven is so deaf he cannot hear the discords he writes." We have to try and distinguish in contemporary music between what is new and worth hearing and what is merely formless noise, with no genuine claim to the name of music.

So it is not easy to pick out the masters, the major composers from the minor composers, when many are still alive and writing, and the babble of sound competing for our attention can easily confuse discrimination.

Also as well as "modern" experiments there are other strong strains in the music of this century. Many composers have looked backward. Folk music is revered. Sixteenth-century music has been rediscovered, and so has medieval music, into which many composers have dipped for refreshment and inspiration.

Yet perhaps the most striking development in the twentieth century is the new pre-eminence of what used to be called light or popular music. Pop music is considered elsewhere but long before that was christened, ragtime and jazz beat their exciting pulse into the ears of the world, through radio and gramophone, and rippled in influence into the consciousness of musicians everywhere. Old divisions have been broken down. There are many voices, some shrill, striving to be heard. You will have to listen with care: our century's music is fascinating.

SOME OUTSTANDING COMPOSERS

Igor Stravinsky (1882–1971)

Stravinsky
and a scene
from his ballet *The Fire Bird*

Now that Stravinsky's long life is complete, we can try to assess his contribution to twentieth-century music, but, true to his times, he is a man of many styles, and in that can be compared with the artist Picasso.

Stravinsky was born into a musical Russian family, and became a private pupil of Rimsky-Korsakov (1844–1908) in 1907. This provided a stimulus to use Russian "folk" material, but the major opportunities for him were made by Sergei Diaghilev. He was the director of the Russian Ballet, and, after hearing an early work performed, commissioned Stravinsky to orchestrate two pieces by Chopin for the ballet *Les Sylphides*. The success of this led to music for the Russian fairy story *The Fire Bird* in 1910. In 1914, Stravinsky left Russia to live mainly in Paris, and was naturalized as French in 1934.

Petrouchka, the next ballet score, in 1911, was less fantastic, and the characteristics of a twentieth-century composer were emerging clearly. Stravinsky sometimes used instruments harshly. The difference between discord and concord no longer seemed to matter, nor staying in one key. Dissonant clashes abounded. In this work, the so-called "Petrouchka chord" represents two keys sounded at the same time. This is called polytonality, and was also experimented with by Debussy, Ravel and Darius Milhaud (1892–1974). Roughly, it is as if Stravinsky played white keys with his right hand while his left played black.

His next work was a sensation. There was a riot of fury from the Parisian audience when *The Rite of Spring* was first performed in 1913. Today, the brutal rhythms of the sacrificial rites seem exciting. Then the primitive music which Stravinsky said was suggested by ideas of earth worship, and celebration of spring after harsh Russian winters, was profoundly shocking. The huge orchestra seemed to be making literally uncivilized noise, a savage attack on their ears. It seemed barbaric then: today it seems innovatory.

During the First World War (1914–18), Stravinsky wrote on Russian themes. He became interested in American jazz, composing *Ragtime* for eleven instruments (1918) and *Ebony Concerto* for dance band.

Then Stravinsky's genius took a new direction. He turned back to the eighteenth century, to Pergolesi (1710–36) and to Mozart, and in the ballet *Pulcinella* and the opera *The Rake's Progress* adopted a neo-classical style. This style was anti-Romantic, using a modern tone of voice to present again the classic forms and patterns. The 1923 Octet for Wind Instruments showed this well.

Stravinsky's aim was to be rid of all influences which were not purely musical. He even asked that certain piano works should be played "without expression", that is without emotional feeling made evident.

Again Stravinsky trod new ground, and in his later works, such as *The Flood, Sacred Ballad*, in Hebrew, and *Elegy for J. F. Kennedy*, he experimented with atonal writing, that is, music not in any key.

From this there arose the twelve note technique which had been invented by Schönberg (1874–1951), in which all twelve notes within the octave (all the seven white and five black notes on the piano, C to C) are considered *equal*. The twelve notes are placed in a particular order or *note-row*, and only used in a dictated pattern, without repetition of one note, until all have been used up. Briefly, that is the method called serialism. It is severe, and full of dissonance, and is typified by the work of Webern (1883–1945), also, like Schönberg, from Vienna, and the music of Berg (1885–1935).

Not only Stravinsky, who became an American citizen in 1945, but many other composers, such as the American Aaron Copland (born 1900) in his Piano Quartet, William Walton in his Violin Sonata, and Britten in his opera *The Turn of the Screw* have made some use of the twelve note series.

All these varied styles and influences make Stravinsky a representative twentieth-century figure. He embraced new lands, new horizons, absorbed differing influences and made them his own.

His long working life is also illuminated by his own writings and sayings, and already by several biographies. Many people are still alive who knew him, saw him conduct and work on records, and still argue about him while he lies peacefully, perhaps hearing only the lapping of water round an island in the Lagoon of Venice.

Serge Prokofief (1891–1953)
Dmitri Shostakovich (1906–75)

These two Russian composers have both suffered from official disapproval and constraint under the Soviet régime, yet Prokofief settled in Russia after a period abroad, and Shostakovich remained in his home country. Prokofief has written a great deal, including a neo-classical *Classical Symphony*, and the popular story with music, *Peter and the Wolf*, operas, ballets and concertos.

Shostakovich has written operas, ballets and chamber music. Listen to his 'Cello Sonata (Opus 40), which gives a good "flavour" of his music.

Ralph Vaughan Williams (1872–1958)
Gustav Holst (1874–1934)

Vaughan Williams' English character is seen most obviously in his love for native folk music, the folk dance movement and his study of Tudor church music. These influences saturate his music, though occasionally it can be harsh in tone.

His friend, Holst, was a teacher as well as composer, as is his daughter Imogen Holst (born 1907). His best known work is the orchestral suite *The Planets* (1918), but it is also interesting to note that Holst early in this century was much interested in the thought and music of the East, and composed the short opera *Savitri* based on an Indian story.

Both these composers worked to produce an English music which was not overpowered by German traditions.

William Walton (born 1902)
Michael Tippett (born 1905) and Others

Walton has worked mainly traditionally, but in *Façade* produced for reciter and instruments a witty and jazz-influenced set of pieces later made into a ballet. His choral works include the cantata *Belshazzar's Feast*.

Michael Tippett (born 1905) has written operas, symphonies and concertos.

These two are followed by a new generation of composers, including Malcolm Williamson (born 1931, in Australia), Richard Rodney Bennett (born 1936) and John Tavener (born 1944).

Some attractive composers whose work you might enjoy include Peter Warlock (1894–1930) for beautifully set songs, either wistful or rumbustious, and sometimes influenced by sixteenth- or seventeenth-century styles. Look out for French piano music by Francis Poulenc (1899–1963) and Gabriel Grovlez (1879–1944).

Benjamin Britten (born 1913)

Britten has a voice of his own. It has an English accent, and yet can speak eloquently to the whole world, as in the *War Requiem*. He has learnt from his English teachers, Frank Bridge (1879–1941) and John Ireland (1879–1962), but most of all from Henry Purcell, whose work he has edited, borrowed from and taken to his heart as a composer for the voice.

Benjamin Britten has contributed immeasurably to English musical life, as a co-founder of the Aldeburgh Festival, a conductor, pianist and composer. With his operas, such as *Peter Grimes* (1945), *Let's Make an Opera* (for children), *Owen Wingrave* (first for television), *Death in Venice* (1973), and small scale church operas such as *Noye's Fludde* and *The Burning Fiery Furnace*, he has totally rejuvenated opera in English. *Curlew River* shows a fascination for Japanese Noh plays.

Technically, he is a brilliant craftsman, and his orchestration is well contrived, with subtle use of percussive sounds. He has not been afraid to write music in the old traditions, and, in a wealth of compositions, has never de-humanized his art with arid experiments. Although his music can be demanding to perform, and sometimes uncompromisingly "modern" in tone, his roots are in East Anglian England, and he does not jet us into mechanical space-age soundings.

Charles Ives (1874–1954) and Some American Composers

It has been suggested that Ives' experiments with separate parts playing in different keys may have been influenced by his youth as the son of an American army bandmaster, hearing two bands at opposite ends of the village green, each playing a different piece! Listen to *The Circus Band* for singers and orchestra with words composed by Ives after the music. A friend suggested that Ives composed like a photographer, including everything comprehensively. He instructed his music copyist not to try to clean it up, because the notes which seemed wrong were right.

Certainly his works were so ahead of their time that he did not gain wide recognition nor many performances until his sixties, but wrote part-time as a pleasure and hobby, to please himself. He also experimented, as Stravinsky did, with polyrhythms, combining more than one rhythm at a time. This is a feature often found in

Charles Ives

primitive African or Indian music. Ives made early use of *tone clusters*, sounding whole blocks of notes all at once. On the piano this might mean using a ruler. His recordings of his own songs are full of a sort of wild musical energy. Yet not all his work was unconventional: he could write in a simple ballad style when he chose.

Samuel Barber (born 1910) has composed in a more traditional, lyrical style. Probably his best known piece is the Adagio from his 1936 String Quartet, which he has orchestrated.

Aaron Copland (born 1900), however, has embraced influences from his native America, especially cowboy songs, Latin-American music and jazz, and has composed in a dissonant non-"popular" style as well.

Virgil Thomson (born 1896) has made use of revivalist hymn tunes in his works, and written much musical criticism.

ADVANCED OR AVANT-GARDE EXPERIMENTS

Perhaps it is to be expected that in a century which has achieved a landing by men on the moon music should stretch out in experiments too. Certainly there have been some wild forays into unexplored regions of sounds.

Music has tried to free itself from earth-bound traditions, and has soared in different directions. Often emotional expression has been replaced by an idea of music being a planned patterning of sounds, to please the brain perhaps more than the ears. Experiments with note clusters using the forearm to press piano keys, or the fingers to pull along a row of strings inside the instrument, and many other new sounds have been tried out by such composers as Edgard Varèse (1885–1965) (born in France, but settling in America), who worked early in this field.

Pierre Boulez (born 1925), Hans Werner Henze (born 1926) and Karlheinz Stockhausen (born 1928) have written in a style which is sometimes fragmented, and strives to combine electronic and traditional sounds into one music.

Chance or Aleatory Music

This goes still further from tradition, and composers like the American John Cage (born 1912), a pupil of Schönberg, have sometimes arranged music in such a way that the performance depends on leaving some parts of it to chance. He has "composed" for example for twelve radio sets and conductor, only specifying loudness, and how much sound and how much silence.

Cage is also well known for his "prepared" piano, which has rubber bands, hairpins and screws attached to its strings.

As well as many contortions within serious music away from the traditional, there have been attempts to join into a Third Stream traditional art music with lighter ragtime and jazz.

As the twentieth century runs its course we have to concentrate to hear its voice clearly. There are many new composers, now working in schools, colleges and universities, able to try out their experiments with budding performers on hand.

Yet originality alone is not enough. It is not enough just to react against the immediate past, for the sake of being startling. Music ne   both artistry and vitality. It must be composed so that when heard it lives for the listener as well as the performer, and says something to both of them. Stravinsky expressed this by saying: "I try to leap a little in spirit." Because of his musical artistry we can follow him.

21 Ragtime, Jazz and Blues

RAGTIME

During the eighteen-nineties, a new kind of music grew up in the Midwest of America, played mostly at first by travelling black pianists in cafés and bars. This was called ragtime, from the syncopated "ragged" time of the treble, set against a steady bass. The syncopation, putting the accent on a weak instead of a strong beat, originated in the rhythms of black African-American music and of the Caribbean too. The relentless beating of the bass was influenced by marching band music and such dances as the polka and quadrille.

Scott Joplin (1868–1917) studied the piano from early childhood, composed and toured cafés and bars, played in a City Concert Band, then in the Maple Leaf Club, which he immortalized in his first composed rag. After some difficulty, this was published in 1899, with such immediate success that Joplin was nicknamed the "King of the ragtime composers". He was a dedicated musician, who returned to college in his thirties to study counterpoint, and was disappointed when his more ambitious operatic works were not successful.

Scott Joplin

Authentic ragtime piano music demands lucid playing. It is good to try out your sight-reading on it, to realize that the apparent inevitability of its steady progress is not as easy as it sounds. Trying to play *Maple Leaf Rag* is a clear demonstration of how simple syncopation works. Joplin instructed on some of his rags: "Do not play this piece fast. It is never right to play ragtime fast."

Later imitators produced a quicker popular version, and Irving Berlin's *Alexander's Ragtime Band* (1911) was a great favourite. In 1914, Joplin wrote his last *Magnetic Rag* nicely subtitled *Syncopations classiques*, for he spiced this perfect miniature piece with a tinge of the European classical composers, like Schubert and Mozart, whom he revered; he remembered the European dances, and he bowed towards the up-and-coming jazz which was to be the new mania to sweep over America and across the Atlantic.

(See record list for the recording by Joshua Rifkin, an American teacher, composer and performer, who has recently "rediscovered" Joplin.)

JAZZ

In the earliest jazz, the player was the composer, and black jazzmen improvised in street marching bands or New Orleans bars. The earliest jazz records were made round about 1916. The style had been developing for some time before the new dance music became known, then widely popular, and taken up by white musicians too.

An outstanding characteristic of jazz is its rhythms, which are based on syncopation. This, of course, had been used earlier by Bach, Beethoven, Schumann, and many others, but the twentieth-century syncopation comes from the work-songs and spirituals of the Negro, in their turn based on primitive African beats. In jazz, the strong accent is dodged by being anticipated or delayed, and irresistibly the listener wants to fill it in, perhaps with his feet. Often the bass beats out in a regular four-four pattern, like a march or hymn, while the upper parts and the tune conflict with poly-rhythms, and so dodge the expected strong accent.

As the jazzman improvised freely on the agreed harmonic basis of a tune, he not only produced cross rhythms with the other

American street band

players, but also dissonant clashes. In addition, blue notes gave the tunes a special quality. They were notes which were traditionally flattened (made lower) by an interval smaller than a semitone in folk music in a way impossible to write down, but easily recognizable by ear, and then passed on to be imitated. There are many people to discover. Listen to the records of "Fats" Waller, Jelly Roll Morton, King Oliver. Some of the solos seem to take wing.

These early bands used saxophones, muted trumpets, trombones, clarinets, the piano, banjo and many percussion devices, some homemade, such as rattles, motor horns, whistles and drums. Sometimes the players would launch into singing, and Louis Armstrong was famous for this.

For Duke Ellington (1899–1974) his instrument was in a sense his orchestra. From the nineteen-twenties he recorded a series of performances which made him acknowledged as the greatest jazz composer, developing his style through a long career. These discs in fact are often the only record of dozens of pieces which were not written down fully or at all, but were improvised by his chosen players for whom they were specially written, or by himself at the piano. Jazz musicians sometimes just write "Con loaf", meaning with your head, when a player is to improvise.

After what is now sometimes called the Trad. or Traditional jazz of New Orleans, there developed a Chicago style, having extended solo pieces as well as the early ensemble with everybody playing together. Benny Goodman (born 1909) was a famous clarinettist and bandleader.

The name swing became popular in the mid-thirties for a simple type of jazz which had a strongly rhythmic and unvarying bass, with a melody improvised above with embellishments. It was ideal for dancing.

George Gershwin (1898–1937) approached jazz from Broadway, as a songwriter. He also composed a symphonic work for piano and orchestra using jazz, and considered by some a hybrid, *Rhapsody in Blue*, in 1924. Then in 1935 he composed a dazzlingly successful Negro folk opera, *Porgy and Bess*.

Achieving commercial success made jazz more standardized, as it sometimes came to be written down rather than created on the spot. But there were many lively offshoots. Styles and fashions shifted frequently.

THE BLUES AND OTHER STYLES RELATED TO JAZZ

From about 1920, there were jazz songs, usually slow and in four time over a twelve bar bass, a sort of sad folk music. A good example is "St James Infirmary Blues".

An instrumental form which is often fairly fast is boogie-woogie, usually for piano or guitar. It often has "a walking bass", a figure which is repeated persistently, rather like the classical *chaconne* and *passacaglia* used by Purcell and Bach. "Beat me Daddy eight to a Bar" of 1940 was typical.

Black Rhythm and Blues from the twenties concentrated on a strong off-beat and by the fifties led to rock 'n roll, typified by Bill Haley's music. Listen to "Rock around the Clock", which alarmed bystanders because cinema audiences literally got up and danced, rocking in the aisles in a way which then seemed madly abandoned. Rock is now a name given quite loosely to pop music with a driving strong beat.

Gospel is black American church music, having characteristic jazz rhythms and mood.

Rebob, becoming bebop or bop from about 1940, began to experiment with new harmonies, and variations on the strict four to the bar beat. The playing of the black trumpeter Dizzy Gillespie was a highlight. Progressive or cool jazz has followed, with a more subdued and complicated style of composition. Instruments new to jazz, such as harpsichords, have been brought into the small serious groups, often of college trained musicians.

True jazz is limited, because it has a fixed background of four beats. Yet it has brought a fresh new idiom into the work of many serious musicians, including early Shostakovich, Stravinsky, Hindemith, Aaron Copland, and Richard Rodney Bennett, who plays jazz on the piano. And, most interestingly, musicians who have best appreciated its character, have tried to bridge the gap, to make a "Third Stream" music, combining established old procedures of composition with the spontaneous and rhythmic liveliness of jazz. The jazz musician, John Dankworth, has experimented and performed in such compositions. Leonard Bernstein has moved freely from one world to the other. Wilfrid Mellers, an English music professor, has written "Yeilichai", a work based on a poem about the Wild West, for chorus, orchestra, jazz trio, soprano, scat singer and electronic devices.

Many musicians now not only enjoy both jazz and serious "art" music, but see the possibility of a fruitful relationship between the two, each learning from the other. Jazz and "straight" playing fused delectably together when the violinist Stephane Grappelli joined with Yehudi Menuhin to play hits of the thirties, such as Cole Porter's "Night and Day", taking it in turn to elaborate the tunes with decorative flourishes, interweaving their individual contributions perfectly.

When asked just what jazz was Louis Armstrong answered: "Honey, you tell 'em if they gotta ask, they ain't ever going to know!" But you can listen. Jazz has many facets to enjoy. Its disjointed step suits our unsettled century, and perhaps appeals to us all the more for that.

Louis Armstrong

22 Pop Music

POP IS MORE than music. For many people it has become a way of life, for some almost a religion. By now a mixture of music, art, entertainment, social life and history, it is worth trying to disentangle some of its roots.

Pop music has been a unique phenomenon because it has been largely created for young people by young people, since the Second World War ended in 1945. Ragtime, jazz, and the formula of the blues taking many forms, had been established in America, first by black, then white musicians too. The idea of singing from the heart was not only applied to black church music, but to the honest expression by a bluesman of his feelings about being African in an American society. Mixed into black American music were remnants of tribal dances, work songs and the "holler" or shout. Early country blues singers like Blind Lemon Jefferson and Robert Johnson had been followed by Lightnin' Hopkins, born c.1915. He built up a great reputation early in the fifties for singing such blues as "Honey Honey Blues" with guitar.

Also there was America's own folk music, Country and Western and Hillbilly. Pioneers made songs of their experiences as they travelled west into a New World, singing with banjo and fiddle "Cumberland Gap", "Wolves Howling" and "Indian War Whoop". Bob Dylan helped to link up the blues with folk music.

All this exploded into American rock 'n roll, first black, but immediately appealing to white young people, who, like Negroes, were wishing to be independent, and to express themselves. Chuck Berry, Bill Haley, Elvis Presley, Little Richard and Fats Domino all developed individual styles within the breakthrough which rock 'n roll represented as the new "beat" dance music, which was physically very exciting, almost hysterical. Phrases of its music did not develop, but were accompanied by an unstoppable beat, almost inducing a trance as people danced.

The Beatles: Merseyside Beat

This intense delight in rock 'n roll beat prepared the way for Beatlemania, the frenzy of adoration which surrounded a group of Liverpool teenagers, John Lennon, Paul McCartney, George Harrison and Ringo Starr, the Beatles, from 1962. They had been playing their guitars and drums in Liverpool clubs with dozens of other small groups, following the earlier craze for do-it-yourself skiffle groups.

The term skiffle was probably first used in Chicago in the nineteen twenties, to describe a makeshift kind of jazz group, which played the washboard, jug, paper and comb or anything that could be banged or blown alongside the standard jazz instruments. In England, early in the 1950s, small skiffle groups playing a mixture of jazz and folk became very popular. Lonnie Donegan, a banjoist, guitarist and vocalist, led in this style.

The Beatles

The Beatles wrote their own songs and words, and seemed to be making a distinctly new sound when they came to public view with unusually long hair and loud confident music, unsentimental and tough in tone, but defiantly gay as well. Other pop music had come from America. With the Beatles, Great Britain had something to say for itself. The impact of their brash beat was immediate. Dancers could feel the rhythm vibrating from the floor up through their own bones. They could pick out a strong rumbling bass line.

The influences on the Beatles' music were varied. As Liverpool is a port on the river Mersey, sailors came in frequently with the

latest blues and rock records from America. There is a large black population, and also an Irish contingent to contribute its folk music. Country and Western music was popular in Liverpool as the Beatles grew up. The music halls still were alive, with song and dance routines which were sometimes copied in singing and street games by schoolchildren. In the Liverpool streets working men's bands processed, and so did the bands of the Loyal Orange Lodge of Protestants with fifes and drums, sometimes clashing with Catholic processions.

That was the Beatles' abundant musical background. Their wit was wry and they mocked themselves frequently. Bob Dylan's songs of protest like "Blowin' in the wind" and "Times They are a-Changin'" were introducing words which had something special to say, reflecting the feelings of a generation.

The Beatles did not merely churn out rock numbers but many types of songs and lyrics: dreamy love songs like "And I Love Her", the rueful "Ticket to Ride", mystifying songs like "Lucy in the Sky with Diamonds", semi-nonsense like "We all Live in a Yellow Submarine", and touching words like the refrain about "all the lonely people" in "Eleanor Rigby". Their lyrics were freshly intelligent, sometimes poetic, and the music matched, drawing on many styles and musical ideas.

George Harrison in particular became interested in Indian music, and learnt to play the sitar. In "Within You Without You", his lyric floats on an Indian drone, played by an Indian tabla (drum) and sitar, so that it merges into the atmosphere of an oriental incantation. The words express what the Beatles were then feeling: that with love the world could be saved, and in time people would merge together, and let life flow through them and round about them.

The music captures the fascination of east for west, blending them in a way which has influenced many other groups.

This song came from "Sergeant Pepper's Lonely Hearts Club Band", a specially coordinated, extraordinarily mixed collection, with its words printed. The whole recording came to be considered a work of art, reviewed seriously, and showing distinct musical development.

The Beatles' music became a world-wide craze. They were mobbed and imitated, embodying the greatest glamour of the pop

Pop singer

world in their progress from cellar clubs to enormous wealth and success in a few years. They made several films, and concentrated on recordings rather than live performance, but finally broke up and now work separately. Their music demonstrates the restlessness of pop. Constantly it searches for something new, swallowing up everything it can find to mould a music for which a giant audience is hungrily waiting.

For pop has brought enormous commercial profits. The sales of thousands of records have been manipulated by many kinds of publicity. Top pops of the week and the month and hit parades have been published and broadcast to promote the sales of records and still more records. Radio programmes pump out pop endlessly, choosing, praising, looking for novelty and sometimes turning the production of pop music into a sort of elaborate party game.

Rhythm and Blues

This followed the early Beatles' work, and was a more primitive and aggressive music, coming from American city blues, as in the work of John Lee Hooker and Muddy Waters. Mick Jagger's fierce vocal style with The Rolling Stones demonstrated this, as did the songs of The Animals, and the work of The Who. A more calm and reflective style also emerged, and was sometimes called soul.

All the way through the fifties and sixties hundreds of groups, with as extraordinary names as they could invent to catch the promoters' ears and eyes, were trying out new combinations of instruments, styles and songs. Audiences numbered in thousands gathered at pop festivals lasting for days to hear old favourites and new hopefuls perform live, their music amplified colossally. In the sixties many youthful rebels, not wishing to conform to society, chose instead to live a life of vague general love and "flower power", treating their pop heroes as priests.

Yet also at the same time pop could be an intensely personal and private experience for some people, their chosen cult. It was not merely a story of pop stars' sensational headlines but of listening to the albums of pop groups. Such works were more than a group of songs, but related numbers with a coherent theme, drawing on a mass of influences, experimenting endlessly. Pop was progressing from danced songs to music for listening. This "turned people on" or "sent" them without leaving their own rooms for a theatre or church or hall. They had the experience of a shared ritual whenever or wherever they could switch on their own music and let it speak to them. Such collectors' passion was almost fanatical.

By their late records the Beatles were trying to convey to such listeners a philosophy set to experimental music. They made use of a string quartet and a wide variety of material. The Who attempted a recorded rock opera called *Tommy*, and there have been full length rock musicals such as *Jesus Christ Superstar*, as composing groups have tried to extend themselves and give their work real form. *Quadrophenia* by The Who has been a more ambitious work still, with seventeen linked songs telling the story, the four musicians having worked for months with synthesisers to produce their final music.

Pete Townshend of The Who is one of the musicians whose experiments cause the development of "progressive" pop to be compared with the work of such "serious" avant-garde composers as John Cage and Stockhausen. They share an interest in amplified instruments and electronics, in *choosing* and prolonging sounds, and you can hear this in pop works by Pink Floyd, Jimi Hendrix and The Mothers of Invention.

Also performers are crossing from one style to the other, to find variety and new life. For instance, the Japanese percussionist Stomu Yamash'ta has claimed that he sees no essential difference between classical, jazz and pop music, and that no barriers should exist. He was trained in classical music in America, and before he was twenty-one had more than twenty concertos dedicated to him by such composers as Henze and Maxwell Davies.

He has composed film music, and can play at a battery of more than fifty instruments, such as drums, gongs, and vibraphones, revelling in the large range of musical expression. When Yamash'ta discovered jazz, he formed his own jazz group, then an ensemble called East Wind. With these musicians, including his wife, a classical violinist, he has produced a pop which blends jazz improvisation with rock, and dazzling orchestral sound. Some of his performances have really been "sound spectaculars" with

Yamash'ta wearing a waist-length red wig.

Another percussionist, Carl Palmer, has been known to bang huge gongs and drums while tolling a large bell in his teeth! His group, Emerson Lake and Palmer, typify two qualities of pop today. First, their sources are so varied, nothing is excluded: Bach, Aaron Copland, ragtime, Hubert Parry, jazz, rock, classical organ music, the Beatles, and much else. Second, there is a new taste for spectacular showmanship. Pop is often now presented accompanied by batteries of lights flashing and flickering round the performers, fireworks and slide shows. A concert becomes a "happening", and experience for vast audiences of being immersed in sometimes almost deafening sound.

Gary Glitter, whose sequinned clothes are torn at by fans in spite of many bodyguards, has even started his act on a silver "Chopper" bike accompanied by motor cyclists revving in time to his rock 'n roll numbers.

In fact, rock 'n roll has already been revived. Some rock groups, like Genesis, are now adding theatrical miming and costumes to their live acts, to give them extra entertainment value. David Bowie uses his personal magnetism to promote rock; Alice Cooper wears extraordinary make-up, and carries a pet snake as he performs. Cuteness and loudness are contributed by very young performers.

Often the life of a pop singer is very short. Names come and names go. Yet still pop is drawing into its net new instruments and styles. Ancient and modern fuse in a "medieval rock band" called Gryphon, whose members, two of whom studied clarinet and bassoon, play the crumhorn, recorder, harmonium, mandoline, bassoon, guitar as well as drums. They plunder early music, and have composed for Shakespeare's *The Tempest*.

Another new sound which has found its way into pop is reggae, the West Indian beat music with a pounding dancing rhythm.

Of course, not only has pop swallowed up African styles, Eastern styles and anything to enhance its relentless beat, but, by its widespread broadcasting it has created new audiences, who are now creating their own pop. So, for example, Greek pop music combines jazz, western pop and Greek folk music with the traditions of music of the Middle East.

Perhaps pop is mostly temporary music, on a small scale, which should not try to grow into large works, but be content to please, and to express the mood and style of succeeding generations. Today it exists in a confusingly varied "scene", with countless performers struggling for recognition and large rewards. Sometimes it is hard to separate the music from the publicity, but if you choose your programmes and look out for reliable reviews rather than sales talk, you will find some music to appeal at once, to enliven and refresh you. Some records will be worth hearing more than once, some worth buying to keep, if a group has something musical to say to you. And probably, when you are old, you will have a special affection for your favourite pop records of today. They will bring back these years at the touch of a switch.

At its worst, pop is a mind-pulverizing, debased exploitation of sound for commercial gain. At its best it is an enticing kaleidoscope of many musics.

Reggae

23 Music for Entertainment

MUSIC HAS ALWAYS been adaptable to the time and place of its performance, to gatherings which are solemn or lighthearted.

The twentieth century tends to be more informal than ceremonial in attitude. Yet for such ceremonies as royal coronations, inaugurations and funerals, music retains its ancient power to heighten the sense of occasion. Processions to music gather to themselves an impressiveness which comes from the music reinforcing the rhythmic movement of people.

The ear and the eye are both attracted by well drilled soldiers marching to a military band. Other processions are helped along by drums and kazoos, fifes or a full blown brass band. Amateur brass bands such as Mills' Bands in the north of England also enjoy concert giving. Joining in a performance of music by beating time, walking, marching or dancing, gives special pleasure to people who cannot play instruments but want to be involved.

Traditional English dancer
with cow's head,
and Morris dancers

MUSIC FOR DANCING

The ancient Greeks and Romans used dancing in religious rites and so do Indians in Hindu temples, and whirling dervishes in Islamic ceremonies to chanting flutes, drums and cymbals, and reading from the Koran.

Sometimes only the priests have danced; at other times, as in many Old Testament stories, the people joined in as when "they sang one to another in dances, saying, 'Saul slew his thousands, and David his ten thousands'."

Always it has been a natural impulse to move to music, to enjoy it with your body. For instance, the American Indians and Mexicans used dancing as a social entertainment and also to mark, with drum rhythms and dancing, the movement of the seasons or the death of a tribesman.

Folk dances reveal the dancing of the common people, and still are nurtured by enthusiasts today, who keep alive, for instance, the old English Sword Dances, Morris Dances, Country Dances and Barn Dances.

Children have kept up their own skipping and dancing songs,

Barn dance

merely altering the words slightly in different districts and from generation to generation. Many nursery rhymes are dancing games.

THE INFLUENCE OF DANCE ON MUSIC

Music has stimulated dancing, but also dances have influenced music enormously. Probably the need for a regular rhythm, phrases which balance each other, contrasted and repeated sections, all giving *form* to instrumental music came from dances.

In courtly society, dances which became fashionable were often used later on as the basis for instrumental works. Among these were the sixteenth-century *pavane* and *galliard*, *bourrée*, *gavotte* and *sarabande*. Later in the seventeenth century country dances became popular, and then were joined in the eighteenth century by the minuet. During the nineteenth century, the waltz, polka and mazurka came into their own. Chopin was making exquisite piano pieces from his national Polish dances.

Our century has witnessed many dance crazes: ragtime and jazz, people jiving and now jerking blissfully to the big beat of pop. Such popular dance music has of course permeated music which is meant for listening. Some concert music is so rhythmically exciting it is perhaps surprising that the audience does not get up and dance to the orchestra.

The Masque

Masques started as aristocratic entertainments, combining singing, dancing, poetry, mime and spectacle. Some of these elements are found in the ballets and operas you can see today. They probably originated as masked processions of musicians and riders who visited noble households, performed, then mingled with their hosts in dancing.

By the seventeenth century, Italy and then England had brought masques into the theatres, and elaborated them with scenery and fantastic "machines", which transported gods and goddesses into scenic clouds, and made the spectacle as important as the music.

Ballet

During the late sixteenth century in France an entertainment grew up, influenced by Italy, which was a combination of masque

From the ballet
The Sleeping Beauty

and ballet. By the reign of Louis XIV a tradition of spectacular dance entertainment was established. Lully wrote music for court ballets within operas, including therefore singing. The King founded a Royal Academy of Dancing, and established such lasting authority that even now most dancing terms are in French.

Ballets left the court and went to theatres. Famous dancers of the eighteenth century introduced new steps and costumes, while the music was borrowed from opera and other music. During the next century, music was written especially for ballet with great effect, for instance the French Delibes' *Coppélia* of 1870. Ravel wrote *Daphnis and Chloë* (1909), Falla *The Three Cornered Hat* (1919), Tchaikovsky *Nutcracker*, *Swan Lake*, *The Sleeping Beauty*, and Stravinsky his magnificent scores.

Many of these pieces have been arranged for concert performance. Ballet in its turn has borrowed music from piano works, from jazz, from Bach and from electronic compositions to accompany its varied styles.

Inspired teachers such as the American, Martha Graham (born 1893), have developed new disciplines with the dancers bare-footed, using a formidable technique. Since 1930, she has been one of the leaders of the Modern Dance movement, choreographing over a hundred dances and ballets.

There have been wide-ranging experiments, matching a more fluid approach to dancing. As in the composition of music, classical restraints and customs have often been put to one side while new forms of expression are explored.

OPERA
Opera too has shaken off many old set forms, and abounds in experiments. You can read more about it on pp. 22–23.

MUSIC HALLS
Perhaps the audiences who now enjoy spectacular musical shows once would have been content with the simpler attractions of the music halls for light entertainment.

These developed from the early London concerts of the seventeenth and eighteenth centuries, taking the form of supper rooms, where a chairman introduced musical "turns" to people as they

Modern ballet

sat at their tables. This saloon theatre developed into the chains of halls, where people paid to enter the Alhambra, the Palace of Variety and other such plush theatres, and heard singers, comic and serious, and orchestras, musicians playing giant organs, glasses, the spoons and other novelties.

It was the cinema which became the halls' deadly rival, and helped their decline. Now they are revived as "olde-tyme" music hall, while the cinema struggles in competition with television.

Many singing stars became immensely popular, and made songs their own, while sharing them with the thousands of people who warbled them in drawing rooms at musical evenings, or whistled them on the streets. Songs like "Home, sweet home . . . There's no place like home", and "Daisy, daisy, give me your answer do. I'm half crazy all for the love of you", could be hummed or sung by anyone with ease. And music hall comedians specialized in funny song-and-dance acts, sometimes inviting the audience to join in lusty choruses.

THE MUSICAL
The name musical came to be given to plays with music given a great deal of prominence, often with large "set pieces" on the stage, and accompanying choruses and dances. Jerome Kern's *Showboat* (1928) was a good example. Some of its songs such as "Ol' Man River" and "Can't Help Lovin' Dat Man of Mine" are still well known from recordings and revivals on the stage and screen. Films also provided their own dancing musical classics with stars like Fred Astaire.

Richard Rodgers and Oscar Hammerstein 2nd combined to produce a series of successes including *The King and I*, *South Pacific*, and *Oklahoma!* The vitality, attractiveness and exuberance of their singing and dancing was a cheering tonic. The magnificent staging of American musicals carried their music far abroad.

They have been revived and filmed, as has Bernstein's *West Side Story*, a version of *Romeo and Juliet*. Dickens as well as Shakespeare has been used as the basis of a musical. Unexpected sources have been tapped. The form is such popular entertainment that there have even been revues based on the lives and songs of Noel Coward in *Cowardy Custard*, and Cole Porter, who wrote twenty-six musicals, in *Cole*.

HOW MUSICIANS ENTERTAIN
THEMSELVES TODAY

Boundaries are less evident in music today. The world has seemed to shrink because travel is so fast, and similarly speedy is the movement of music. Broadcasting and recording make new music and new performances available immediately all over the world.

Films of performers being taught, practising as well as playing, bring the intimate study of music making into people's homes. The lives and works of composers have been recreated on the screen for television and cinema audiences.

Other opportunities have widened. Regional, national and international youth orchestras and bands flourish and multiply. Music is often written specially for young performers who may sing, dance and play in a gathering of a thousand, or practise devotedly in chamber music schools and camps.

Rigid divisions between types of music, even the new classifications in youthful pop are being forgotten when for instance classical musicians try out a composition or make a record with friends from pop or jazz. The guitarist John Williams, who has made such excursions, has, to broaden the scope of his playing, also helped to found a musical ensemble of seven instrumentalists including an Indian tabla and a Japanese koto. They play works written specially for them, and arrange pieces by such composers as Vivaldi.

It seems likely that many composers and performers will continue to enjoy working within traditional frameworks, and music tomorrow will partly be what we hear today. Yet also experiments will be carried forward. We shall learn to accept new sounds, and composers will gradually distinguish between real progress in their art and blind alleys leading nowhere.

The voice of music can make its own contribution to international friendship. It speaks a language which can bridge gaps in understanding, and lead to a sharing of technical and artistic experience which is valuable for both sides.

The voice of music can be a delight and consolation to you for the rest of your life, if you learn to listen now.

Musical Terms

A SHORT LIST of the most common forms in which music has been composed. See the Index and the list for further reading for fuller reference.

Cantata
: A work originally for accompanied solo voice, and now commonly for voices with instrumental accompaniment. The subject can be religious or secular.

Chamber music
: Music for two (duet), three (trio), four (quartet) or more instruments, originally intended for playing in private houses. Each player's part is of equal importance.

Concerto
: In modern usage, a concert piece displaying the skills of one or more instrumentalists in conjunction with an orchestra. Usually this is in several movements.

Concerto grosso
: An older form of concerto in which a small body of solo instruments alternates and contrasts with a larger group of players.

Fugue
: A piece written for a fixed number of parts or voices. Each one follows the other in stating the "subject", which is a short tune or motif. This tune may be developed or changed, and appear in different keys, as the parts speak and answer.

Opera
: A dramatic work set to music and performed on stage, with solo and choral singing as an essential part, even if some dialogue is spoken.

Oratorio
: A work, often religious in subject, for soloists, choir and orchestra, usually performed in a church or concert hall.

Quartet
: A piece of music composed for four singers or players. For example, the string quartet is for two violins, viola and 'cello, the piano quartet is for three bowed instruments and piano. The forma of a quartet is similar to that of a sonata.

Sonata
: A small-scale instrumental work for one or several instruments which, by the eighteenth century, had become a piece usually in four movements: a quick, a slow, a lively one such as a minuet, then a fourth quick movement.

Suite
: A set of instrumental pieces, often based on dances, and often all in the same key.

Symphony
: A major work which is a version of the sonata for full orchestra. Sometimes the movements are linked together by similar musical material, or one idea or subject.

A SHORT LIST of the most commonly used terms to direct the speed or tempo of playing, how loud or soft it should be, and with what expression. Traditionally, they are usually given in Italian.

Accelerando, often shortened to *accel.* — quickening the tempo

Adagio — slow and leisurely

Allegro — quick and lively

Andante — moving along fairly slowly

Appassionata — passionately

Assai — very

A tempo — in time, back to time after slowing or hastening the speed

Con brio — with vigour, spirit

Con expressione — with expression

Con fuoco — with force, passion

Crescendo, cres. — becoming louder

Decrescendo, decres. — becoming softer

Dolce — sweet

Forte, f. — loud, strong

Fortissimo, ff. — very loud

Fortepiano, fp. — loud, then immediately soft

Grandioso — magnificent, grand

Largo — broad, dignified

Lento — slow

Meno — less

Mezzo-forte, mf. — half loud, neither loud nor soft

Mezzo piano, mp. — half soft, fairly soft

Moderato — moderately fast

Molto — much

Morendo — dying away

Non troppo — not too much

Piano, p. — soft, quiet

Pianissimo, pp. — very soft

Più mosso — with more movement, quicker

Poco a poco — little by little, gradually

Presto — nimble, quick

Rallentando, rall. — gradually slower

Ritardando, ritard. — gradually slower

Ritenuto, rit. — held back

Sempre — always

Sforzato, sf. or sfz. — marked with forceful accents

Sostenuto — sustained, held on

Tempo primo — the first or original speed of playing

Tempo rubato — in "robbed" time, with one part played slower or faster, then "paid back", lingering and hurrying

Tenuto, ten. — held on

Vivace — brisk, lively

Record List

Bach, *Goldberg Variations.* Landowska, harpsichord. RCA VIC 1650.

———, "Favorites." Biggs, organ. Columbia MS 6261.

Beatles, The, "Sergeant Pepper's Lonely Hearts Club Band." Capitol SMAS 2653.

Beethoven, Ninth Symphony (the "Choral"). Soloists, Chicago Symphony Orchestra, chorus, Solti. London CSP 8.

Bernstein, "Leonard Bernstein Conducts His Music for the Theater." New York Philharmonic, Bernstein. Columbia MG 32174.

Brahms, Clarinet Quintet. De Peyer, Melos Ensemble. Angel S–36280.

Britten, *A Young Person's Guide to the Orchestra: Variations and Fugue on a Theme of Purcell.* Britten, London Symphony. London 6671.

———, *Noye's Fludde.* Soloists, chorus, English Chamber Orchestra, Del Mar. Argo ZNF 1.

Chopin, Mazurkas. (complete, 6 sides) Rubinstein, piano. RCA LSC 6177.

———, Polonaises. (complete, 4 sides) Frankl, piano. Turnabout 34254/5.

Copland, Aaron, "Copland Conducts Copland." Columbia M30649.

Debussy, *Prélude à l'après-midi d'un faune.* Suisse Romande Orchestra, Ansermet. London STS 15109.

Delius, *On Hearing the First Cuckoo in Spring.* Hallé Orchestra, Barbirolli. Vanguard S240.

Dvorak, Ninth Symphony (*From the New World*). New York Philharmonic, Bernstein. Columbia MS 6393.

Dylan, Bob, "The Times They Are a-Changin'." Columbia KCS 8905.

Elgar, Cello Concerto In E Minor. Tortelier, London Philharmonic Orchestra, Boult. Angel, S-37029.

Ellington, Duke, "The Golden Duke." (4 sides) Prestige 24029.

Gershwin, George, Excerpts from *Porgy and Bess* and *An American in Paris.* Philadelphia Orchestra, Ormandy. Columbia MS 7258.

Grieg, Piano Concerto. Entremont, Philadelphia Orchestra, Ormandy. Columbia MS 60616.

Haley, Bill, "Greatest Hits." MCA 161 E.

Handel, *The Messiah.* soloists, Alldis singers, London Philharmonic Orchestra, Richter. (6 sides) Deutsche Grammaphon 2709045.

Hopkins, Lightnin', "Roots." Folkways 31011 E.

Ives, Charles, "17 Songs." Jan de Gaetani. Nonesuch 71325.

Joplin, Scott, "Piano Rags." Rifkin. Nonesuch 73026.

Lloyd Webber, Andrew, and Rice, Tim. *Jesus Christ, Superstar.* Original cast. 2MCA 10000.

Monteverdi, *L'Orfeo.* Concentus Musicus, Harnoncourt. Telefunken 3635020.

Mozart, Fifth Violin Concerto. (The "Turkish".) Heifetz. RCA LSC 3265.

Prokofiev, *Peter and the Wolf*. Ustinov, Philadelphia Orchestra, Ormandy. Angel S–35638.

Rolling Stones, "Big Hits." London NPS 1.

Schubert, *Die Schöne Müllerin*. Fischer-Dieskau. Deutsche Grammaphon 2530544.

———, *Der Erlkönig*. DG 2530229.

Stockhausen, *Gesang der Junglinge. Kontakte*. Deutsche Grammaphon 138811.

Stravinsky, *The Rite of Spring*. Columbia Symphony Orchestra, Stravinsky. Columbia MS 6319.

Tchaikovsky, Excerpts from ballet suites, *Sleeping Beauty* and *Nutcracker*. Royal Philharmonic Orchestra, Boult. Seraphim S60176.

Vaughan, William, "Greensleeves," "Fantasia on a Theme by Thomas Tallis." "The Lark Ascending." Brown, Academy of St. Martin-in-the-fields, Marriner. Argo ZRG 696.

Verdi, *Aida* excerts. Price, et al. London Symphony Orchestra, Leinsdorf. RCA LSC 3275.

Wagner, "An Introduction to *The Ring*." Soloists, Vienna Philharmonic Orchestra, Solti. London RDN 5–1.

Walton, *Facade*. Sitwell, Pears, English Opera Ensemble, Collins. Odyssey 32359.

Collections.

Dunstable, Josquin de Pres, "Motets," Purcell Consort of Voices. Argo ARG 681.

Gibbons and others, "High Renaissance Music in England." (madrigals) Purcell Consort of Voices, Jaye Consort of Viols. Turnabout 34017.

Granados and others, "Julian and John." Julian Bream, John Williams (guitars). RCA ARL 1 0456.

Gregorian Chant, Plainsong. Carmelite Priory Choir. London McCarthy. Oiseau 60040.

Menuhin, Yehudi, and Grapelli, Stephane, "Jalousie: Music of the Thirties." Angel S–36806.

"The Nonesuch Explorer" Music from Distant Corners of the World; Treasures of the Explorer Series. (2 records Sampler). Nonesuch H 7–11. (There are 60 in the series, covering different cultures and areas of the world, ask your librarian or record dealer for specific titles.)

Shankar, Ravi, Concerto for sitar and orchestra. Shanker, Previn. Angel S–36806.

UNESCO, Regional Anthology of Folk and Traditional Music. May be ordered from Peter's International, Inc., 619 West 54th Street, New York, N.Y. 10019. For example: Bengal CO 641/7840; Cambodia CO 641 7841; Ivory Coast CO 641 7842; Portugal CO 641 7843.

Books for Further Reading

The Voice of Music is an introductory book, and probably the best way to find more books is to look up subjects or musicians in your nearest library. It is worth remembering that libraries often have books which can no longer be bought, because they are out of print.

For general reference:

Scholes, Percy, *The Concise Oxford Dictionary of Music,* 2nd edition, ed. John Owen Ward. New York, Oxford University Press, 1964.

————, *The Oxford Companion to Music,* 10th edition. New York, Oxford University Press, 1970.

————, *The Oxford Junior Companion to Music.* New York, Oxford University Press, 1954.

Baines, Anthony (ed.), *Musical Instruments Through the Ages.* New York, Walker, 1975.

There are many biographies of musicians, but it is worth looking out for the "Great Composers" series, including:

Holst, Imogen, *Bach.* New York, T. Y. Crowell, 1965.

————, *Britten.* New York, T. Y. Crowell, 1966.

Other recommended books:

Baker, Richard, *The Magic of Music.* New York, Universe, 1975.

Berger, Melvin, *The Violin Book.* New York, Lothrop Lee & Shepard, 1975. (also: *The Flute Book; The Clarinet & Saxophone Book.*)

————, *The Story of Folk Music.* New York, S. G. Phillips, 1976.

Bernstein, Leonard, *Young People's Concerts.* New York, Simon & Schuster, 1970. (out of print)

Boni, Margaret Bradford, *Fireside Book of Folk Songs.* New York, Simon & Schuster, 1947.

Britten, Benjamin and Holst, Imogen, *The Wonderful World of Music.* Garden City, N.Y., Doubleday, 1968. (out of print)

Bulla, Clyde Robert, *Stories of Favorite Operas.* New York, T. Y. Crowell, 1964. (also: *More Stories of Favorite Operas; The Ring and the Fire.*)

Collier, James Lincoln, *Inside Jazz.* New York, Four Winds Press, 1973.

————, *Which Musical Instrument Shall I Play?* New York, W. W. Norton, 1969. (out of print)

Dietz, Betty Warner and Olatunji, Michael Babatunde, *Musical Instruments of Africa.* New York, John Day, 1965.

Ewen, David, Mainstreams of Music series: *Opera* (1972); *Orchestral Music* (1973); *Solo Instrumental and Chamber Music* (1974); *Vocal Music* (1975); *Composers of Tomorrow's Music: Ives, Schoenberg, Webern, Bouley, Varese, Stockhausen, Xenakis, Babbit, Cage, & Partsch.* New York, Dodd, Mead, 1971.

Headington, Christopher, *The History of Western Music.* New York, Macmillan, 1976.

Hemming, Roy, *Discovering Music: Where to Start on Records and Tapes, The Great Composers and Their Works, Today's Major Recording Artists.* New York, Four Winds, 1974.

Rublowsky, John, *Music in America.* New York, Macmillan, 1967.

Shanet, Howard, *Learn to Read Music.* New York, Simon & Schuster, 1956.

Shankar, Ravi, *My Music, My Life.* New York, Simon & Schuster, 1968.

Wechsberg, Joseph, *The Pantheon Story of Music for Young People.* New York, Pantheon, 1968.

Young, Percy M., *Music Makers.* Roy (distributed by Ventura Book Service, Rockaway Park, N.Y. n.d.).

Index

Page references for main entries are shown in italic, eg *123*.
Page references for illustrations are shown in bold, eg **234**.